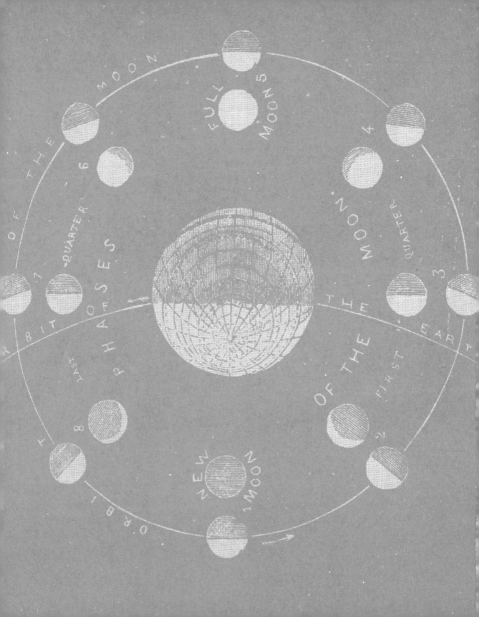

The
Good Witch's Guide

A MODERN-DAY WICCAPEDIA OF MAGICKAL INGREDIENTS AND SPELLS

Shawn Robbins and Charity Bedell

STERLING ETHOS
New York

STERLING ETHOS
New York

An Imprint of Sterling Publishing Co., Inc.
1166 Avenue of the Americas
New York, NY 10036

ISBN 978-1-4549-1952-0

Distributed in Canada by Sterling Publishing Co., Inc.
c/o Canadian Manda Group, 664 Annette Street
Toronto, Ontario M6S 2C8, Canada
Distributed in the United Kingdom by GMC Distribution Services
Castle Place, 166 High Street, Lewes, East Sussex BN7 1XU, England
Distributed in Australia by NewSouth Books
University of New South Wales, Sydney, NSW 2052, Australia

For information about custom editions, special sales, and premium and corporate purchases, please contact
Sterling Special Sales at 800-805-5489 or specialsales@sterlingpublishing.com.

Manufactured in Canada

6 8 10 9 7 5

sterlingpublishing.com

Cover design by Elizabeth Mihaltse Lindy
Interior design by Sharon Jacobs, with Ashley Prine, Tandem Books

PICTURE CREDITS — *see page 307*

Dedicated to Leanna Greenaway and Charity Bedell,
the wind beneath my wings.

—Shawn Robbins

)✦(

Firstly, this book is dedicated to the ancestors. Those who have
gone before and who are now a part of the land we live on.
Among those is my grandmother, Francis Caouette.
Secondly, this book is dedicated to the teachers who saw
something special in me: Mrs. Spencer, Mr. Dudley, Mr. Lawson
(may you rest in peace), and Mr. Robinson. They all believed in
and encouraged me to develop my skills and talents as a writer.
They all believed I'd be published someday.

—Charity Bedell

Contents

Part One

YE OLDE WITCH'S WISDOM, RITUALS, AND FORMULAS

Part Two

SPIRIT SPELLS AND SPIRITUALITY

Part Three

CRAFT YOUR OWN PERSONAL MAGICK

Appendix

$\mathcal{A}$uthors' $\mathcal{N}$otes

SHAWN ROBBINS

My name is Shawn Robbins, and I am an author, a psychic, and a paranormal researcher. The journey that led me to explore the unexplained, the strange, and the unknown and took me into the world of medicine, magick, and miracles began when I was a young girl growing up in Queens, New York.

My grandparents were immigrants from Russia and Hungary. They came to the United States penniless. But they brought with them on their arduous and long boat journey to America something far more precious than what money could buy: bottles filled with dried herbs, oils, and botanical medicines to cure their ills. In the Old Country village where my grandparents lived, surrounded by dense forests as far as the eye could see, they did not have access to doctors when they got sick. The closest doctor was literally hundreds of miles away. Instead they had to rely on the local healer, called "the medicine man" by the villagers, whose knowledge of plants and herbal medicine was their only source of healing.

After my grandparents arrived in America, those same bottles of botanical medicines, dried herbs, and oils would become lifesavers for my mom, and for me as well. You see, they arrived in 1916, when the great polio epidemic was raging in New York City. Over six thousand Americans died from the dreaded and incurable disease. When my mother was born a few years later, she became afflicted with this feared illness. Gram did not have the money to seek a doctor's help, but she did have an excellent working knowledge of botanical medicine. She made broths and teas from plants to help Mom recover. Many months later, Mom rallied and was left with only a slight tremor in her arm.

The next polio epidemic happened in the 1950s, and a young doctor by the name of Jonas Salk invented the first polio vaccine. I was among the first to receive the vaccine, but within hours I became ill with polio. The live virus had been insufficiently inactivated in some batches of the vaccine, and the batch I got was one of them. I was hospitalized for some time, but what doctors could not cure, Gram's tea did. I was polio-free after ten days of drinking her herbal brew—with no lasting effects from the polio.

You could say that being ill and hospitalized brought about the epiphany that changed my life, because until then one of my childhood dreams had been to become a doctor and help heal those with incurable diseases. After I recovered from polio, though, I spent most of my youth reading books on holistic medicine and botanical remedies. Edgar Cayce, who has been called "the father of holistic medicine," became a go-to source for information on healing. But my greatest source of knowledge was my family. My grandparents and mother regaled me with the history and folklore of medicinal plants and herbs and taught me how to use them in everyday life.

In my early twenties, I met two of the most important people in my life: Bryce Bond, a well-known healer, and Timothy Green Beckley, founder of the New York School of Occult Arts. They would help me realize my childhood dream of helping the ill and infirm. Once Bryce and Tim learned of my interest in holistic medicine, they introduced me to the greatest healers from around the world. These renowned and respected healers taught me about the laying on of the hands, psychic surgery, magnetic healing, meditation, and all things related to helping heal the mind and soul, and, subsequently, I went on to teach the art of holistic medicine and healing at Tim's school.

Still, I sensed that my life was incomplete. Coming from a psychically gifted family and with my own gift to see into the future and read minds, I knew that there was more in life to learn and explore. Call it fate or kismet—I met the noted parapsychologist Hans Holzer, who took me under his wing. He used hypnosis and magnetic energy to help me develop my psychic powers even further. For example, I foresaw the MRI machine before its development in 1971 (as noted in several of Hans's books, including *The Prophet Speaks*).

This book is the culmination of all my knowledge and research. I fervently hope that you will become inspired and empowered to heal yourself and others. Real healing power is within every one of us. Always remember: your body is a temple. Nourish it, and take care of it; in return, it will take care of you.

CHARITY BEDELL

My name is Charity Bedell. I have been practicing witchcraft for seventeen years. While I was raised in the United Church of Christ, a Protestant denomination, my mother encouraged discussions of spirits, angels, and even taught me about the saints. My father taught me to respect nature (Mother Nature and Father Sky) and about the Great Spirit who encompasses all of nature and humanity. When I reached my teen years, I began to wonder why the church didn't teach about Mother Nature and the Great Spirit, and why the earth was not really respected.

My journey into witchcraft started on my thirteenth birthday, when I was given Silver Ravenwolf's *Teen Witch* as a gift. Once I learned that there is a spiritual path connected to the land, as well as angelic forces, gods, and a multitude of other spirits, I knew I was home. Everything that both my parents had taught me was found in witchcraft in some form. I had a goddess (Mother Earth) and a god (Father Sky) as well as the creative force (Great Spirit).

Living in Maine today, I am surrounded by nature. My path uses a variety of shamanic techniques, trance work, prayer, meditation, and offerings to connect to the spirits of the land. Walking in the woods, on the beach, or taking a hike in the mountains refreshes me and helps me feel alive. My witchcraft is wild and free, just like the wilderness of Maine.

Over the years I have studied and explored many different styles of witchcraft and paganism. My current path is a mixture of Germanic paganism and traditional witchcraft. Germanic paganism provides a context for honoring my ancestors and their gods (Norse/Anglo-Saxon). Traditional witchcraft allows me to connect with the spirits of the land, as well with as my ancestors.

Currently, I am a student of Valerie Walker (aka Veedub) in the Feri tradition of witchcraft. I have also studied with Christopher Penczak and am a dedicant in the Temple of Witchcraft tradition. I have taken workshops at events with numerous other witches, including Raven Grimassi and Orion Foxwood. These teachers have been wonderful mentors, helping me grow and develop as a witch.

I believe strongly that all magickal and spiritual paths have something to teach me. I am always exploring and learning new routes. Currently I am studying conjure (hoodoo) with Starr Casas. Other magickal interests include Nordic folk magic (trolldom), runes, Enochian magic, druidry, kabbalah, shamanism, ceremonial magic, and Egyptian magic (Heka).

My path to alternative healing and herbalism, much like my path to magick, is tied to my youth. Growing up, I dealt with attention deficit/hyperactivity disorder (ADHD), as well as digestive issues, depression, and social anxiety. My mother was very much into holistic health practices, and, with her guidance, we treated those issues with herbal supplements and dieting. When I was sick with a cold, I would take an echinacea supplement to boost my immune system before using cough syrup. If I had an upset stomach, oftentimes I would drink peppermint tea.

While my mom made changes to my diet and gave me herbal supplements, I explored magickal options for treating my depression and anxiety. Through witchcraft, I learned the skills of aura reading, soul retrieval, and chakra alignment, as well as general tools to contact and communicate with spirits. I used these abilities to treat my depression and anxiety. In doing so, I learned that my path was to help people heal the spirit, as well as the mind and body.

Now I use herbs spiritually in my practice. My path to being a magickal herbalist began when I learned that most of the incenses I was burning were synthetic and causing headaches and breathing problems for my fiancé. With that knowledge, it was off to the local New Age, metaphysical shop to buy herbs and make my own incenses. Today I am a magickal and spiritual herbalist. I craft incenses, powders, tinctures, oils, and ritual baths. I use spiritual and magickal aromatherapy for almost all my magickal practices and treat my own depression and anxiety by using herbal baths and incenses that I create. With the help of the gods and the spirits, I have learned a lot. With the support of my family, in the summer of 2013 I was able to open a shop where I sell my handcrafted incenses, oils, tinctures, baths, and much more. Mystic Echoes has been a dream come true, enabling me to share my knowledge of magickal herbalism with the world.

Working on this book has been another dream come true, giving me a new way to share my knowledge of holistic health and herbalism. There is so much out there to learn and explore. Writing this book has helped me learn more and develop further as an herbalist, and I hope it helps you learn and grow as well.

Preface

We are each on a unique journey to find inner peace in our everyday life. To get there, some of us take a road less traveled, while others follow the tried and familiar path. But no matter what road you are on, the destination, or goal, is to make yourself whole.

It is our aim to inspire and empower you with knowledge that will assist you in reaching your goal, to guide you with witchy tips from yesteryear—coupled with modern-day magickal tips—to help you learn and grow. After all, as a reader of our book, you are the most important person in the world to us. You are someone who is willing to try new things, from using holistic medicine to help you feel better emotionally and physically to using candle magick and ancient spells to increase your awareness that all things you wish for and want in life are possible—if only you believe the real power is within yourself.

In the chapters ahead, you will come to understand how faith and magick play an integral part in your own life. We can provide the tools to help you get there, but before you take that first step in crossing over the bridge to wisdom, you must ask yourself: What is it that you are seeking in life? Power over your personal circumstances, emotional stability, self-awareness? We see you and hear you in your personal quest and hope to provide you with the answers which—or witch—you seek.

As witches, we believe that it is okay to be yourself and follow your own journey through learning without being judgmental. It is true to say that we are all different, but in the end, we all become one. We are all connected to a higher universal force.

Our book endeavors to bring out the best in you by exploring different aspects of holistic healing and how it relates to your overall well-being. Have you ever experienced a panic attack, extreme stress, insomnia, or digestive complaints? Any one of those problems can cause additional physical symptoms in the body, such as muscle stiffness or tension headaches. This is not to say that your symptoms are not real; they may be manifestations of a larger problem that can be helped through alternative healing coupled with witchy wisdom and magick.

We hope that, as you read through each chapter of our book, you take away insight and knowledge to help you turn your weaknesses into strengths. It is our belief that oils and botanicals, proper diet and nutrition, spells and chants, and time spent outside in nature all work together to put you in tune with your inner and outer being, to bring serenity and peace. As above, so below; as within, so without. May the gods, goddess, and spirits bless you on this journey.

SPELLCASTING 101

Before you dive into the details, we want to discuss the basics and key tenets of spellcasting. No matter what the spell is or how it is performed, all spells and methods have one requirement in common: *intent*!

If a spell is to be successful, its essence must derive from deep within the caster, which is where the spell gains its power. All that is needed is a true belief that what you are about to do will have the desired effect. If you have even the smallest amount of doubt that it won't work, then you will likely be disappointed. Your spell may only half work, or the outcome may be distorted. It is thought to be very similar to cosmic ordering (a philosophy similar to the law of attraction, which advocates that the power of positive thinking can invoke change), so it involves true self-belief and a great deal of mind over matter. You truly have to believe that your spell will work and have confidence in yourself as a caster to get positive results.

Mental Focus

We display physical energy by being active and mobile. It's safe to say that some of us have more vigor than others, but what many people don't realize is that, just as we possess physical energy as human beings, we also maintain mental energy. We can't see or touch this mental energy because it is completely invisible to the human eye, but even so, we hold this mysterious power and use it every day. Mental energy is potent and can affect our emotions and the emotions of those around us. We are usually able to sense when someone is happy or sad or angry, even if their body language or expressions do not automatically convey their mood. Some people believe that you can experiment with mental energy by staring at the back of someone's head, testing to see if they sense someone watching them and turn around; or by concentrating on someone to see if they will contact you. These are examples of projected mental energy, and it's the very thing you need to make a spell work best!

Our mental strength is just as dynamic as our physical strength, and it is transmitted by a combination of concentration and focus. When working with magick, it is vital that we center ourselves and become completely engrossed in the outcome of what we want to achieve. We can improve our mental energy and focus, training it and strengthening it like a muscle, which can help increase the power and success of our spells.

It is not completely clear how spells work, but the theory is that, by focusing with powerful intent, you create an invisible energy "ball" that is sent directly to either your deity, if you have one, or straight out into the universe. We know relatively little about the universe, but we are all part of a grand design, and every living thing on Earth is connected to the universal force in some way. You don't need to have a specific faith for a spell to work, but it is thought that during a spell, the message sent by the caster is received by a higher power and granted accordingly. It's a myth that you have to be a witch in charge of a broomstick to cast out energy in the form of a spell. Anyone can do it! Some consider it to be like the power of prayer. If you are sending out an affirmation of what you need or desire, then someone or something will come to your aid and make it happen. You just have to find the path that suits you best and believe in the outcome.

Saying a spell repeatedly helps to enforce the message, which, in turn, gives it more power each time it is spoken. Generally, a spell is recited no less than three times in a row.

Traditional or Modern Witchcraft

WHICH SPELLS ARE BEST?

There are thousands of spells in circulation today. Some are tried and tested ancient rituals passed down through generations. Others have a more modern background. Years ago, witches relied on local healers or covens to obtain the information they required, or they had to source old battered spell books in dusty bookshops just to learn some Wiccan wisdom. We are so lucky that today we have access to the Internet. With the click of a mouse, we can find a wealth of knowledge at our fingertips, from all corners and cultures of the world. Reading lots of literature from all perspectives is a good idea. Whether you prefer to access traditional sources, or you find yourself fancying modern-day magick, both methods work equally well. You simply have to find what feels right and resonates a truth within you.

Although there are many variations of traditional witchcraft in the world, the rules can be inflexible, and spells are thought not to work unless certain preparations are followed exactly. To cast a successful spell using the traditional magick, an altar has to be used at all times and must face a certain direction depending on the time of day or the season. The cardinal elements, such as earth, air, fire, and water, have to be present on the altar, and the tools and moon phases must all correspond with the spell at hand. (*Note: In the Northern Hemisphere, the element earth is associated with north, air with east, fire with south, and water with west.*

In the Southern Hemisphere, air and water keep their directions, but earth is south and fire is north.)

For example, in the Northern Hemisphere, a bowl of salt, the sign of a pentagram, and green candles would all be positioned north of the altar. Red candles, an athame (ceremonial dagger), and anointing oils would all be situated south. Water, a chalice, and blue candles would be placed to face west, and incense, a bell, and yellow candles would all face east. The correct god or goddess must be summoned in order to bring success, and hard-to-find herbs are the very ingredients needed for the spell to work. The list of potential materials is endless! (You will find an abundance of information online regarding the specifics of traditional spellcasting, including the whys and hows of which objects are represented by which directions.)

Lots of practitioners today have a far more laid-back approach. In reality, modern Wiccans have found that we don't need all these hard-and-fast rules and boundaries in place to cast the perfect spell. By no means are we disparaging the ancients or how they cast their magick, but the belief today is that a thought is a living thing that enables us to bring about our desires without most of the paraphernalia that has been traditionally suggested. It is true that there are tools we can use to enhance our magick and a wonderful supply of flowers or crystals can give our spells more potency, but we can comfortably perform a spell on the kitchen worktop instead of an altar, or if we are in a busy environment, we can simply recite a rhyme of positive intent to bring about an effect.

The bottom line is this: lots of spellcasters today still love the old, conventional methods. There is nothing wrong with feeling that you need a traditional ceremonial setting to work your magick, but for those who live in the fast lane, spellcasting on the fly works in a similar way and is just as effective!

CONSEQUENCE AND PERSONAL GAIN

There are two different types of spellcasters: those who work with positive energy and those who work with negative energy. From a Wiccan point of view, there is one definite rule of thumb: what you send out, you get back threefold. Given that tenet, most casters only perform a ritual with good intent.

Another way to think of this is that when you perform your ritual, the magickal ball of energy you are sending out into the universe will at some point return to you, its creator. If your spell was for blessings and happiness for others, you will go on to receive them too, in some way or another. But if it is to perpetuate pain or control another person, the unpleasant power you have conjured will swing back around and hit you head-on. This in turn can cause a succession of bad luck, ill health, or worse! This is called the bounce-back effect, and it's very real.

Another rule that a true Wiccan follows is not to perform magick to change a person's free will. This concept can cause a cloud of confusion. Differentiating between what desire is for personal gain and what is for the greater good needs to be considered properly before any magick is attempted. It is very tempting to change the behavior of someone who is causing you grief, but is it ethically correct?

Let's say your teenager is being obnoxious. It is quite acceptable to spellcast for him to be more amenable. At the end of the day, if he is calm and less obstinate, he is likely to be more content. If that is truly your intent, then you have the best interests of your child in mind, and this is an acceptable use of spellcasting. This can also be acceptable if you have a vicious in-law or a bully for a boss. You would be creating a happier environment for all concerned, as well as making your life a little easier, if you caused that person to be less combative or critical. Because you are casting magick for the greater good, ethically speaking, it's not crossing over any forbidden boundaries. (There is always a possibility, though, that you may not know the full story about any given situation [see chapter 6, page 154]; therefore, this kind of spellcasting should be approached with care and extra thoughtfulness.)

However, let's imagine now that you desperately want a promotion at work and you know another colleague is earmarked for it. By casting a spell in hopes of causing your boss to pick you and not your colleague, you would be meddling with your boss's free will and changing the outcome of something that may not have been meant for you in the first place. You would in turn change the destiny of the other person who was meant to have the promotion, and then your karma could be seriously affected.

Rules are also in place with regard to affairs of the heart. Never cast spells to win the love of another person. It is okay to cast a general spell for love—this allows the universe to speed up the development of affections in any person who would be spiritually intended for you—but specifying a particular person could change the course of destiny and have disastrous consequences.

My general advice is to keep your thoughts grounded. Think very carefully before you begin a spell, and make sure you are not conjuring up your heart's desire for your own personal gratification. Defining personal gain is not easy, but with any kind of spellcasting, you have to first ask yourself whether you *want* what you're conjuring, or if you *need* it. For example, most people don't think they have enough money to live on, so one of the first spells they are likely to cast is one to win the lottery. Sadly, this type of spell falls into the "personal gain" category. You might want more money, but do you really need it? The answer to that is probably not!

Money spells are allowed, but usually, if you cast spells for cash, you will only receive the exact amount you may need for a specific bill—not a huge windfall. This means lottery or gambling spells hardly ever work. Money magick does work brilliantly when you need an extra few hundred dollars to pay an unexpected bill, or you want to start a new project but have no means to fund it. But if you want to win the jackpot or bet on a winning horse, we are afraid you will be disappointed!

You also have to consider fate and destiny. Most Wiccans believe that things in our lives happen for a reason, so if you are meant to follow a certain path in life and if it is your destiny to do a certain thing, no amount of spellcasting is going to change it. For example, you might be determined to find new employment, so you cast a specific spell for the job of your dreams. If your spell doesn't work and you don't get that job, it is highly likely that you were never meant to have it in the first place. It is when we look back over time that we realize the things we desired would have led us down a different path and we wouldn't be where we are today. With spellcasting, you have to keep an open mind and accept that you can't always conjure exactly what you're asking for. Yes, you can make things happen, and yes, you can change your life in some small ways, but when certain things don't transpire, it's either because you didn't have the right intent and belief that the spell would work, or it was never meant to be!

As above, so below; as within, so without. May the gods, goddess, and spirits bless you on this journey.

Part One

Ye Olde Witch's Wisdom, Rituals, and Formulas

Chapter 1

Barefoot in the Magick Garden

THE HISTORY AND FOLKLORE OF MAGICKAL HERBS AND SPICES

Mr. and Mrs. Pagan knew that when you felt ill, you wanted to get well. They had a fire in their bellies and a passion to heal the sick and infirm in their community, and they worked their magick with age-old remedies and cures that were passed down to them from their ancestors—from one generation to the next. The tenets and principles they followed still hold true today.

Our ancestors looked to the plants that grew in their local forests and gardens to heal their ailments. Knowledge of healing plants—and of what to mix together to address fevers and aches and to stop infections—was the province of the local healer or wise one in the community. Some of these practices we know today as herbal remedies—like drinking peppermint or ginger tea to help with stomach issues. But how did these people first learn of the healing nature of plants and which herbs to use for specific ailments?

By watching animals find and eat certain herbs and by observing what happened when animals touched or ate plants like poison ivy, ancient herbalists were able to learn from nature which plants were good for what issues. Over time, herbalists developed a large knowledge base of herbs and plants to use in diverse situations.

This knowledge was applied to magickal as well as physical healing work. To the ancient world, there really was no separation between mind, body, and spirit. They were all connected. What affected one aspect of your life (not having a successful crop, for example) could affect your mental health, physical body, and spiritual well-being. So spells for prosperity and success would focus on all aspects of the need.

The fact that ancient cultures were so dependent on understanding the cycles of nature allowed herbalists to observe and develop their craft. By watching nature, they could see when it was best to plant and when it was best to harvest. They knew which plants worked best fresh and which ones were best dried. Herbalists knew the local plants that were native to their area.

Nowadays, the herbal tradition is being revived by people who look to nature to address health and wellness issues.

THE DOCTRINE OF SIGNATURES

Magickal and spiritual herbalists often rely on a principle called the doctrine of signatures, which dates back to medieval folk medicine and basically holds that like affects like; something that has the appearance of a particular thing can cure that particular thing. For example, the plant eyebright has flowers that resemble the shape of an eye, so it was used to treat problems related to sight. Spiritually, this lead to eyebright being used in rituals related to psychic sight or to enhance mental abilities.

Early herbal medicine relied heavily on the doctrine of signatures. In the early days of the Christian church, it was often said that "God made it so we would know what to use the plants for."

This knowledge was most often passed from teacher to student or parent to child. Most of the herbal practices in ancient and medieval times were transmitted orally because the majority of people could not read. Training included harvesting herbs, preparing them, and administering them, as herbalists also learned through practical application and experience.

Many items used by medieval herbalists are still utilized in medicinal and magickal herbalism today. Eyebright is still used for ailments of the eye, and lungwort is still used by some herbalists to treat ailments of the lung. Some more modern herbal essence remedies, such as the Bach flower remedies—developed by the British doctor Edward Bach in the 1930s—use a variation on this doctrine. Bach focused on the vibrational and energetic aspects of plants and other substances rather than on their visual appearances, and sometimes the results were just as good.

A WORD ABOUT SAFETY

Before we talk about how to practice herbal medicine and work with natural alternative medicines, it is important to think about safety. There are many herbs that contraindicate conventional medications. St. John's wort, for example, is known to be an excellent herbal supplement to address depression; however, it has also been known to counteract the effects of many different forms of birth control. Because some herbs can cause severe adverse effects for certain medical conditions when taken with certain medicines, if taken in combination with other herbs, or if taken before or after surgery, knowing what you can use and what you can't is vitally important.

It is also important to remember that, when it comes to herbal medicine, the U.S. Food & Drug Administration (FDA) considers them to be dietary supplements "not intended to treat, diagnose, prevent, or cure diseases." Additionally, "federal law does not require dietary supplements to be proven safe to FDA's satisfaction before they are marketed." (See www.fda.gov for more information.) This should not stop you from using alternative medicine or herbal supplements, though. They can be wonderful healing tools and great additions to a healthy life. You just first need to check with your doctor, do your research, and ask questions of a certified herbalist or a medical professional trained in herbalism.

All this being said, there are plenty of ways to use your own simple remedies. Making salves, teas, and ointments are great starting points. Just remember that if you experience any adverse effects, immediately stop your treatments and seek help from a trained medical professional.

THE PATH OPENS

The planet we live on is full of medicinal plants, whether you find them in your garden, your yard, or in the wild. Learning to work with the plants and herbs in your own backyard and local to you can help you live a healthier life and be more connected to the world around you.

Combining magical and medicinal herbalism is a practical path. There is a lot that a person can do with items that they have in their own home. Just by looking in your spice cabinet, in your pantry, and out the window at your lawn, you can find ingredients to create many different remedies and spells that can be crafted and performed right in your own home without the need to travel or buy expensive ingredients.

It is important to remember that the health of the body and the health of the spirit are connected. While many people in the modern world do not take this for granted, historically it was generally accepted. Many treatments used in the past dealt with spiritual aspects of an illness as well as the physical symptoms, as it was believed that many ills were caused by spirits or demons within us. For example, plants such as garlic and onions were considered to have both exorcism or banishment potential, as well as healing properties.

Witches believe in this connection between the mind and the body and will use magick and rituals to help deal with the spiritual aspects of health care. Some of the healing work a witch does will be in the form of rituals, while other aspects will involve herbal supplements, teas, or decoctions. It has been shown that the power and associations of the mind influence the health and wellness of the physical body. When something affects the mind, the body and spirit are also affected. Some ailments like depression and anxiety do more damage to the mind and spirit than to the body, but all three are connected.

COMMON FOLK REMEDIES

Now, where do we begin? Let's start by looking at the folklore and folk remedies of our ancestors. Long ago, people were unable to simply drive down to the local pharmacy or grocery store to get medicine when they were sick. These people had to rely on remedies that they could make at home using what was available in their garden or the environment. They found remedies for almost everything, from headaches and stomachaches to fever and coughs, and many are simple treatments that can be created quickly and easily. They are not only effective, but they may also save you lots of money in the long run. Some of them can be used right after they are prepared, while some need to sit overnight in a fridge or container.

One ingredient used often in folk remedies that has a lot of health and healing potential is honey. There are good reasons why honey is included in numerous cough medicines, cough drops, and lozenges. Raw honey has natural antibiotic properties that help kill off harmful bacteria. It is also a natural sweetener that not only tastes good—just a tablespoon will soothe the pain of a sore throat. Honey helps prevent coughs and laryngitis. By coating the throat, it prevents irritation, which helps make speaking and breathing easier.

Apple cider vinegar is another great ingredient. If you eat a starchy or carb-rich meal and take some vinegar while eating, the vinegar will feed the good bacteria in your gut, helping with digestion and constipation and boosting your immune system. Apple cider vinegar is very acidic, so it should not be taken straight or it could damage the enamel on your teeth and your esophagus. Take one tablespoon diluted in a small glass of water as needed. (Check with your health-care professional before starting regular use, especially if you have diabetes.)

ANGLO-SAXON FOLK CHARM

The Nine-Herb Charm (from the *Lacnunga* codex, a collection of Anglo-Saxon texts compiled around the eleventh century) is a very powerful Anglo-Saxon charm/spell in the form of a poem. Originally pagan, over time it came to contain both Christian and pagan elements, and it is possible that a Christian monk recorded the poem for history. This charm/spell, which covers nine sacred and special herbs, is intended to heal infections and be an antidote to poison:

Remember, Mugwort, what you made known,
What you arranged at the Great proclamation.
You were called Una, the oldest of herbs,
you have power against three and against thirty,
you have power against poison and against contagion,
you have power against the loathsome foe roving through the land.

And you, Waybread*, mother of herbs, / open from the east, mighty inside.
Over you chariots creaked, over you queens rode, / over you brides cried out,
over you bulls snorted. / You withstood all of them, you dashed against them.
May you likewise withstand poison and infection
and the loathsome foe roving through the land.

Stune** is the name of this herb, it grew on a stone, / it stands up against
poison, it dashes against pain. / Nettle it is called,
it attacks against poison, it drives out the hostile one, it casts out poison.
This is the herb that fought against the serpent,
it has power against poison, it has power against infection,
it has power against the loathsome foe roving through the land.

Put to flight now, Venom-loather***, the greater poisons, / though you are the lesser,
you the mightier, conquer the lesser poisons, until he is cured of both.

---

*Plantain
**Watercress
***Betony(?)

Remember, Chamomile, what you made known, / what you accomplished
at Alorford, / that never a man should lose his life from infection
after Chamomile was prepared for his food.
This is the herb that is called Wergulu.* / A seal sent it across the searight,
a vexation to poison, a help to others. / It stands against pain,
it dashes against poison, / it has power against three and against thirty,
against the hand of a fiend and against mighty devices,
against the spell of mean creatures. / There the Apple accomplished it
against poison / that she [the loathsome serpent] would never dwell in the house.
Chervil and Fennel, two very mighty ones. / They were created by the wise
Lord, / holy in heaven as He hung; / He set and sent them to the seven
worlds, / to the wretched and the fortunate, as a help to all.

These nine have power against nine poisons.
A worm came crawling, it killed nothing.
For Woden took nine glory-twigs,
he smote the adder that it flew apart into nine parts.
Now these nine herbs have power against nine evil spirits,
against nine poisons and against nine infections:
Against the red poison, against the foul poison,
against the white poison, against the purple poison,
against the yellow poison, against the green poison
against the black poison, against the blue poison,
against the brown poison, against the crimson poison.

---

*Crab apple

Against worm-blister, against water-blister, against
thorn-blister, / against thistle-blister, against
ice-blister, against poison-blister. Against harmfulness of the air, against
harmfulness of the ground,/ against harmfulness of the sea.
If any poison comes flying from the east, / or any from the north, or any from
the south, / or any from the west among the people.
Christ* stood over diseases of every kind. / I alone know a running stream,
and the nine adders beware of it.
May all the weeds spring up from their roots,
the seas slip apart, all salt water, / when I blow this poison from you.

Mugwort, Waybread open from the east, Stune, Venom-
loather, Nettle, Chamomile, Wergulu, Chervil and Fennel,
old soap; pound the herbs to a powder, mix them with the
soap and the juice of the Apple.

Then prepare a paste of water and of ashes, take Fennel,
boil it with the paste and wash it with a beaten egg when
you apply the salve, both before and after. / Sing this
charm three times on each of the herbs before you (he)
prepare them, and likewise on the Apple. And sing the
same charm into the mouth of the man and into both his ears, and
on the wound, before you (he) apply the salve.

*Woden (?)

The Nine-Herb Charm is an effective set of folklore that lists nine useful herbs in healing. The charm gives you instructions on how to perform the spell and work the magic. Some of the herbs have changed over the years, as folk names and common names for herbs can fluctuate over time, though the effectiveness of this charm has not diminished with the changes and adaptations.

So here we now have nine different herbs for healing:

MUGWORT (*Artemisia vulgaris*)

PLANTAIN (*Plantago major*)
{called "waybread" in the nine-herb charm}

WATERCRESS (*Nasturtium officinale*)
{Called "Stune" in charm; note that some translations interpret the original Anglo-Saxon as lamb's cress, also known as hairy bittercress (*Cardamine hirsuta*)}

NETTLE (*Urtica dioica*)

BETONY (*Betonica officinalis*)
{Called "Venom-loather" in the charm}

CHAMOMILE (*Chamaemelum nobile*)

CRAB APPLE (*Malus sylvestris*)
{Called "Wergulu" in the charm}

CHERVIL (*Anthriscus cerefolium*)
{in some versions of the charm, wild thyme (*Thymus serpyllum*) is substituted for chervil}

FENNEL (*Foeniculum vulgar*)

It is important to remember that, historically, most herbs and plants were gathered in the wild by the local herbalist. Back then, the typical options for healing materials and food were what could be grown, hunted, or gathered locally. Many of the plants in this charm are considered weeds today (like chamomile, mugwort, and plantain) and so may be gathered wild.

Now let's take a look at the health and healing properties of these nine herbs individually. This will serve as a starting point for working with herbs for health and healing in everyday life. Once you get the hang of it, healing with herbs and natural alternatives can be a fun and easy way to take control of your own health and healing.

Mugwort (*Artemisia vulgaris*)

Mugwort is the first herb mentioned in the Nine-Herb Charm. We can see that mugwort is one of the oldest healing herbs known to the Anglo-Saxons. The phrase "against contagion" means that the herb works well against fevers and sicknesses. "Power against the loathsome foe" shows that the herb has protective properties as well.

One example of mugwort folklore involved gathering it on St. John's Eve (June 23) and wearing the sprigs as a crown. It was said that wearing a mugwort crown on this day would protect the wearer against illness, disease, and misfortune and also protect against evil possession. Avoid mugwort during pregnancy and breastfeeding.

Plantain (*Plantago major*)

The second verse of the charm introduces the herb "Waybread," which has been identified as plantain. This is a very hearty plant. The charm illustrates in detail how this plant can survive abuse of all kinds. Plantain has naturally occurring antibiotic properties, referred to in the charm as the ability to withstand poison and infection. These antibiotic properties are why plantain is commonly found in natural salves and ointments that are used to treat open wounds.

While this herb is not commonly used magickally, it still has magickal potential. It works well for calling on your own inner strength. It can be used in healing spells to ward off illnesses. If it is used to help someone who is already ill, it can build up the person's strength to fight the illness.

Watercress (*Nasturtium officinale*)

The next herb mentioned in the charm is "Stune" or watercress. The charm notes that "it stands up against poison, it dashes against pain." We can see that the Anglo-Saxons saw it as an antitoxin and an analgesic. There are many nutrients in this herb, and it was commonly used in tonics. Additionally, this herb is said to have properties that can help with skin care, like when the juice is applied topically.

When it comes to spirituality and magick, this herb is related to the water element. Lore states that it was used to protect people traveling across the water and was carried in red flannel bags. Traditionally, it was also used as a visionary or psychic herb.

Watercress should be avoided when pregnant, as it can cause miscarriages. It is also not considered safe for use on small children. Finally, this herb should not be used with certain medications, specifically anticoagulants. So if you are on anticoagulants, nursing, pregnant, or planning on becoming pregnant, you should discuss another herbal alternative with your medical practitioner.

Nettle (*Urtica dioica*)

This is a common herb that is often disliked because its leaves sting, causing burning pain and itchiness. However, the herb in the poem is seen as a powerful tool to use against poison and infection. Infections have been a serious threat and a major cause of death throughout history, so it was and is important to know many herbs that could be used to fight infection and keep the body free of illness and disease. Fighting off infection involves boosting the immune system, and nettle does just that (see page 202). Here is a folk spell for healing a fever using nettles:

> Pull the nettle plant up by the roots and recite the name of the one with a fever and their parents' names.

Nettle, like many multifaceted herbs, can be used in a variety of charms. The Nine-Herb Charm gives us three clear uses for the herb in magickal and spiritual work. These are protection, healing, and exorcism (dispelling of forces), with protection charms being one of the best uses of nettle.

Avoid nettle during pregnancy and while breast-feeding. If you have diabetes, kidney issues, low blood pressure, or are on anticoagulant or mood-stabilizing medications, speak with your health-care practitioner before using nettle.

Betony (*Betonica officinalis*)

One herb in the charm that is hard to pinpoint is "Venom-loather." The consensus is that the herb in question is betony, aka wood betony. Historically, it was a common cure-all plant. One theory is that the herb's name comes from an old Celtic words *bew* (head) and *ton* (good), meaning "good for the head." This tells us the herb can be used for headaches and migraines. (If you are taking medication for high blood pressure, check with your doctor before use.)

The charm also describes betony as a powerful herb that can stand up to other herbs, which makes it good for protection. It can also "conquer the lesser poisons, until he is cured of both," making it an element of removal and purification.

Chamomile (*Chamaemelum nobile*)

Of all the herbs listed in the charm, this is the one that most people are familiar with. Its healing properties have not been lost to time. Chamomile is probably best known for its use in relaxation and stress relief. Its calming qualities promote rest, which is key to recovering from any ailment. It is also commonly used for pain relief, including soothing earaches and toothaches. (Note that chamomile may cause interactions with some medications and birth control pills.)

Spiritually and magickally, this herb is used in spells for sleep and dreams, as well as in money-attraction and love spells. It is also said that the sunny disposition of the herb can make it useful against curses and hexes, breaking them with its powerful, uplifting scent.

Crab Apple (*Malus sylvestris*)

The next charm stanza provides much insight into the qualities of the crab apple. One key aspect is its use as a charm to protect against snakes. It also "dashes against pain" and "against poison." Medicinally, the juice of the crab apple is said to be an antiseptic, described in the poem as "a vexation to poison." Other uses include boiled compresses to treat eye irritations and for beauty treatments. Its magickal and spiritual uses include beauty and love spells. There is a reason for the saying "An apple a day keeps the doctor away."

Chervil (*Anthriscus cerefolium*) or Thyme (*Thymus vulgaris*), and Fennel (*Foeniculum vulgare*)

The last three herbs in the charm are listed together: chervil (or in some versions of the charm, thyme) and fennel. This verse is different from the rest of the charm where the herbs are identified individually, suggesting that these herbs work best when paired together.

Chervil is an aromatic herb that has many different healing properties: it can act is a diuretic to help treat constipation and as an expectorant to help relieve coughs and colds. It is also used as an anti-inflammatory and mild analgesic.

There are many species of thyme available; we are focusing on wild thyme (*Thymus serpyllum*), which was likely the species used during the Anglo-Saxon period. Thyme has many useful healing properties. It is antiseptic and is used for treatment of respiratory and abdominal distress, particularly to help deal with problems in the lungs and stomach.

Fennel, with its licorice flavor, is used in herbal concoctions to make their taste more appealing. It is also helpful for respiratory issues and is useful to people who are fasting, because it eases hunger pains and helps stabilize metabolism.

These three herbs also have powerful spiritual and magical properties, making them great plant allies. Growing these herbs in your garden will provide excellent opportunities to bond with them and attune yourself to their energetic properties.

Chervil is a particularly spiritual herb. One of its common uses is for communication with the spirit. Working with chervil will help you gain wisdom and understanding of your true spiritual essence. The best use for this herb is in rituals that deal with death or dying.

Thyme is associated with fairies, or wee folk, and with the dead. Some cultures also use thyme to build courage and ambition. In Greek traditions, it was used for purification prior to any magickal or spiritual work.

Fennel has properties of protection and strength. In some cultures Fennel is thought to protect against black magick. When hung at your windows, it is said to protect and ward off evil spirits.

For those with bleeding disorders, note that thyme might slow blood-clotting. Chervil and fennel should not be used during pregnancy or while breastfeeding.

BACKYARD HEALING

The ten plants mentioned on the previous pages are only the beginning of the journey for herbal healing and practice. While they are a wonderful start, they are not all available everywhere in the wild, and they cannot all be grown by everyone. But there are many other herbs that can be used for healing and magick that you might find (or grow) in your own backyard. Let's take a look.

Dandelion (*Taraxacum officinale*)

This is an herb everyone should be familiar with: the dandelion. All parts of the plant can be used— the roots, the juice, the greens, and the seed tops —and it's a good herb to get familiar with. It is a very hearty plant, and it can grow just about anywhere. Some people eat the greens, and some roast and eat the roots. The young greens make a great salad, and they are very nutritious, too.

Dandelion has many healing uses: it has laxative properties, removes toxins, and helps diminish and clear acne and boils. It also has a few spiritual uses. The most common magickal use is to blow the seeds into the wind and make a wish. Other uses include money attraction, purification, personal and spiritual enrichment, beauty spells, psychic gifts, and psychic development.

Lavender (*Lavandula officinalis*)

Lavender is another common herb that is cultivated in many gardens. It has a beautiful flower with a very pleasant, relaxing fragrance.

Lavender is popular for a few reasons. It has many health, healing, and spiritual uses, and it can be used in incense, oil, food, and tea.

Place a few drops of diluted lavender essential oil on your temples and at the base of the neck to relieve a headache or migraine. The plant's essential oils can also be used to help heal acne or troubled skin, but the most common healing property of lavender is that it fights fatigue.

Spiritually and magickally, lavender is used in many different ways. Sleep and healing spells commonly call for lavender. It is also used to promote peace and love. There are stories about lavender being associated with longevity. Finally, the plant is also associated with protection and cleansing.

Note that certain sedatives or sedative antidepressants may interact with lavender and cause overdrowsiness; discuss with your medical practitioner before using lavender if taking any of these drugs.

White Birch (*Betula pendula*)

This tree has many uses in Native American traditions. The primary healing modality of white birch is as an antiseptic, and it is associated with purification and exorcism.

The *B* rune in the Anglo-Saxon runic alphabet, called *berkana*, stands for "birch," and birch relates to the Mother Goddess and Mother Earth and to the cycles of death and rebirth. This is where the tree's association with the dead and the underworld comes into play.

The birch tree that grows across northern Europe is sacred to many gods and goddesses in the Anglo-Saxon and Germanic traditions. It is also one of the first plants to produce leaves in the spring. In Celtic regions on May Day, or Beltane, celebrants danced around birch maypoles in honor of fertility goddesses. When couples were gifted with a newborn, the placenta was placed under a birch tree as an offering. One of the many deities associated with the birch tree in Nordic traditions is Frigg, the Earth Goddess and wife of Odin. Birch twigs were traditionally used to make witches' brooms, and many cradles were made from birch bark to protect infants, bringing the protection of the Earth into the home. Freya, the Norse goddess whose attributes include love and fertility, is also symbolized by birch. Young boys in love often placed green sprigs of the birch tree around the house of the young ladies they were trying to court.

There is also Thor, the god of thunder, lightning, strength, and fertility. Farmers purified and protected their flocks by gently striking their animals with birch twigs when they went to pasture after the winter. It was believed that if you brought a birch twig struck by lightning into your living quarters, then Thor himself would protect your home.

You can utilize the healing and protection aspects of birch in a ritual to banish or remove illness.

Pine (*Pinus*)

Pine is another common tree. Like many other herbs, pine has different uses depending on the species. White pine is a great expectorant, which makes it useful in cough and cold season. One of the best ways to use it is to drink white pine needles steeped in a tea to help you cough up phlegm when you have chest congestion or a cold. Larch pine, which is common in central Europe, is also considered an expectorant for bronchitis and pneumonia.

Pine trees are said to be sacred to the god Poseidon. Pine sap was used on many ships to keep them waterproof and water resistant. This is probably where the protective aspect of the plant came into play. It is said that holding on to a fresh pinecone with seeds still intact will keep away evil spirits and bring fertility. Pine is also associated with money and work, because it is an evergreen plant, which suggests prosperity all year long. The final associations of pine relate to health and healing, protection, cleansing, exorcism, purification, and fertility.

This chapter introduced some traditional herbs for health and healing, as well as a potent charm that has been passed down through history. Many of these herbs would have been either grown specifically by a local herbalist or wise healer, or gathered and identified in the wild by herbalists. Folklore and folk remedies can be wonderful ways to explore the world around you. Take a look at the plants you grow in your garden or find in the woods. So many plants have medicinal properties, and you can learn from nature.

Chapter 2

Aromatherapy

SOUL-BOOSTING
HEALING ESSENCES

The sense of smell is arguably the most underestimated sense we have, as it can actually be one of our most powerful healing allies. Aromas can trigger pleasant memories—from the smell of cookies baking in the oven to the scent of a loved one's perfume to the fragrance of a flower—as well as unpleasant reminiscences. Aromatherapy is the art of using the power of scent to heal the body, mind, and spirit.

IT ALL MAKES SENSE

Aromatherapy and the use of scent in healing rituals, magick, and spirituality is not a new thing. Humans have always enjoyed the scent of flowers and have long observed the different effects plant odors have on the human mind and body. In the ancient world, the use of the aromatic properties of herbs in healing, magick, and ritual was well known. The ancients understood the connection between the mind and body in health, happiness, and well-being. The ancient Egyptians honored their gods using a variety of incenses and oils, the preparations of which were very ritualized and held deep spiritual meaning. Native American peoples used herbs for spiritual purposes as well as for healing and health. Many cultures still use fragrant herbs in healing rituals and to honor the dead, the spirits of nature, and the divine.

Today, the practice of aromatherapy is once again widespread, and the use of scented candles, bath salts, and potpourris have become particularly popular. Health-food stores carry lines of essential oils and oil blends. Even department stores carry synthetic oils and scented candles. Aromatherapy is accessible to everyone, and it is an effective and simple way to make positive changes to your health in mind, body, and spirit.

PERSONALIZE HEALTH WITH ESSENTIAL OILS

The simplest way to work with aromatherapy is by using individual essential oils. The oils are unique, and many of them have multiple uses. By learning the different uses of each essential oil, you can focus your work on the oils that have the most beneficial effect on your health. While working with individual essential oils, you will discover that some are too strong for you, and others may even produce a negative reaction.

Essential Oils for Health and Wellness

There are hundreds of essential oils on the market. Not all of them have pleasant scents, and not all of them are effective on the skin. The following list provides several common essential oils and the benefits they offer.

ALLSPICE Reduces stress, calms, relaxes tight muscles, uplifts mood, improves digestion, naturally disinfects

BASIL Calms, relieves pain, relieves fatigue, improves mental clarity, purifies the body

CARDAMOM Relieves pain, uplifts mood, improves digestion, improves mental clarity and memory

CATNIP Anti-diarrheal, relieves indigestion, relieves anxiety, uplifts mood

CHAMOMILE Reduces anxiety, promotes restful sleep and relaxation, relieves pain

CINNAMON Relieves pain, uplifts mood, relieves fatigue, naturally disinfects, improves digestion, increases appetite

CLOVE Relieves pain, uplifts mood, improves mental clarity, improves digestion, naturally disinfects

CORIANDER Relieves pain, relieves fatigue, improves digestion, improves mental clarity and memory

EUCALYPTUS Breaks up congestion, relieves pain, naturally disinfects, vapors help with breathing

FRANKINCENSE Anti-inflammatory, antiseptic, astringent, diuretic, improves digestion, expectorant, sedative

GERANIUM Relieves stress and tension, uplifts mood, anti-inflammatory, soothes itchy skin

GINGER Relieves pain, uplifts mood, relieves fatigue, improves digestion, increases appetite

JUNIPER BERRIES Relieve pain, energize, improve mental clarity and memory, anti-inflammatory, repel insects, soothe insect bites

LAVENDER Relieves stress and anxiety, promotes restful sleep, uplifts mood, balances mood swings, vapors help with breathing, improves digestion, naturally disinfects, breaks up congestion

LEMON Balances the nervous system, uplifts mood, relieves fatigue, improves mental clarity and memory, naturally disinfects

LEMON BALM Relieves anxiety and stress, promotes restful sleep

LEMONGRASS Calms, balances nervous system, uplifts mood, anti-inflammatory, vapors help with breathing, improves digestion, naturally disinfects, repels insects

LIME Relieves fatigue, uplifts mood, naturally disinfects, improves mental clarity and memory

MANDARIN Reduces stress and tension, calms, uplifts mood

MYRRH Helpful in meditation, uplifts mood, anti-inflammatory, aids in healing skin

NEROLI AND ORANGE BLOSSOM (both come from blossoms of the bitter orange tree) Remove nervous tension, promotes restful sleep

NUTMEG Relaxes tight muscles, relieves pain, improves digestion

PALMAROSA (a lemon grass genus) Relaxes tight muscles, relieves pain, uplifts mood, helps regenerate skin, anti-inflammatory

PEPPERMINT Relieves pain, uplifts mood, relieves fatigue, breaks up congestion, anti-inflammatory, vapors help with breathing, improves digestion, increases appetite, soothes itchy skin, improves mental clarity and memory

PETITGRAIN (from leaves and twigs of the bitter orange tree) Reduces anxiety and stress, promotes restful sleep, uplifts mood, improves mental clarity and memory

PINE Lessens pain, uplifts mood, relieves fatigue, breaks up congestion, naturally disinfects, improves mental clarity and memory

ROSE Relieves pain, uplifts mood, anti-inflammatory, aids in healing skin

ROSEMARY Relieves pain, stimulates nerves, relieves fatigue, vapors help with breathing, improves digestion, improves mental clarity and memory, naturally disinfects, repels insects

SPEARMINT Relieves pain, uplifts mood, relieves fatigue, breaks up congestion, anti-inflammatory, vapors help with breathing, improves digestion, improves appetite, improves mental clarity and memory, soothes itchy skin

TEA TREE Relieves pain, naturally disinfects, aids in healing skin, vapors help with breathing

THYME Relaxes tight muscles, relieves pain, uplifts mood, breaks up congestion, anti-inflammatory, improves digestion, increases appetite, improves mental clarity and memory, naturally disinfects

YLANG-YLANG Relaxes tight muscles, relieves pain, promotes restful sleep, uplifts mood, naturally disinfects

Practical Sense and Safety

Working with essential oils can be easy, but it is still important to understand some basic safety issues and take reasonable and responsible precautions. After all, not only do you want to work toward better health and wellness, but you also want to be safe.

The most basic safety concern when working with essential oils is about proper handling and storage. First, it is important to dilute essential oils in a carrier oil before using them therapeutically. You should rarely apply an undiluted essential oil directly to your skin. By diluting essential oils in a carrier oil, you not only get more use from your supply of oil, but you can also prevent skin irritations. Common carrier oils are olive, grapeseed, almond, flaxseed, and sesame seed oil. Use $\frac{1}{8}$ cup (30 ml) of carrier oil per 10 drops of essential oil and $\frac{1}{4}$ cup (60 ml) per 15–20 drops.

The next thing you need to consider is storage. Essential oils need to be kept away from light and air. It's best to store oils and oil mixtures in dark or brown bottles. This will keep away light and help prevent spoilage. Most essential oils can be kept for one to two years in proper storage, while citrus oils should not be used after six to nine months.

Before you start to work with essential oils, do a skin allergy test. Many people have sensitive skin, and you may be one of them, so it's a good idea to test your carrier oils. To test for allergies, simply apply a drop of carrier oil to your skin and check to see if there is a reaction within twelve hours. If there is no reaction, add one drop of essential oil to fifteen drops of the carrier oil. Apply the blend to your upper chest area and check to see if there is a reaction within twelve hours. If there is no reaction, then you have no allergy to the oil or the plant.

Finally, some essential oils should be avoided if you have dry or sensitive skin and when you are pregnant or breastfeeding. If you have sensitive skin, it is best to avoid the following essential oils: black pepper, cinnamon, clove, grapefruit, lemon, lemon balm, lemongrass, lime, mandarin, orange, peppermint, and spearmint. If you are pregnant or breastfeeding, avoid these oils: cardamom, coriander, geranium, ginger, grapefruit, lavender, lemon, lemon balm, lemongrass, lime, mandarin, neroli, palmarosa, petitgrain, spearmint, and ylang-ylang.

Scents and Sensibility

When you start working with essential oils to address health issues, begin with just one symptom or issue you would like to heal. Focusing on that, limit your selection to only a few essential oils. Once you have the basics down, you can create your own wonderful oil blends and also determine which are best used as perfumes, in bath salts, or added to melted candle wax at the base of a candle (never add while the candle is lit).

STRESS Several essential oils can be effective for relieving stress. Stress often has side effects, including anxiety, upset stomach, and rapid breathing. One essential oil that works well on stress and anxiety is peppermint. It relaxes the mind and body and helps with digestion. Lavender is another good choice, as it relaxes muscles and the vapors can help regulate breathing.

PAIN AND MUSCLE TENSION Muscle tension is something many of us deal with. When using essential oils for pain relief from muscle tension, the best approach is to create a massage oil to rub into the affected area. If you are trying to relax muscles and ease pain, allspice is an excellent choice. Geranium essential oil is a good alternative—it reduces inflammation and muscle tension and provides stress relief.

CHEST CONGESTION The common cold, the flu, and seasonal allergies can all result in chest congestion, so this ailment can happen at any time of year. To use essential oils to relieve chest congestion, apply a few drops of diluted oil across the chest and massage them into the skin. The best oil for congestion relief is eucalyptus oil, which can break up congestion from coughs, colds, flu, and allergies and helps restore proper breathing. Thyme oil is another excellent choice for relieving congestion.

CONCENTRATION AND FOCUS Everyone sometimes has difficulties with concentration and focus. This can result from a lack of sleep, stress, anxiety, depression, or a reaction to life events. To use essential oils for help with focus and concentration, apply a few drops to the temples, middle of the forehead, and base of the neck. Rosemary is an excellent oil when you need to focus intently or commit things to memory. Spearmint helps relax and calm the mind, which promotes mental clarity.

FATIGUE Many people feel exhausted at the end of the day even if they think they're getting enough sleep. The best way to use essential oils for issues related to energy and fatigue is to apply a few drops to your wrists and rub them in. Lemon or lime oil work great here. Both of them uplift mood, relieve fatigue, and provide mental clarity and focus. Lemon also helps balances the nervous system.

INSOMNIA Many people just can't seem to fall asleep. Apply a few drops of essential oil to your forehead and at the base of the neck and see if the soothing scents relax your mind and body. Lemon balm is an excellent oil for this, as it addresses anxiety and stress and promotes restful sleep. Ylang-ylang oil can also help you sleep, and it relieves muscle pain that may be getting in the way of a good night's sleep.

ANXIETY This is a horrible issue that involves the physical and mental body. Physical symptoms may include anxiety or panic attacks, asthma

attacks, feelings of paralysis, and tremors. Nonphysical symptoms may include clouded thoughts, racing mind, feelings of confusion, and a sense of being disconnected. To treat anxiety with essential oils, apply one drop each to the forehead, base of the neck, wrists, and along the collarbone or upper chest. Chamomile, lavender, and lemon balm are excellent oils for relieving anxiety and relaxing the body.

CRAFTING YOUR OWN OIL BLENDS

The thing to remember about essential oils is that a little goes a long way. They are concentrated forms of the essence of plants, so you need very little to accomplish much. Less is more! One undiluted bottle of an essential oil should allow you to create several blends and treatments.

You don't need much in the way of supplies to make your own essential oil blends. You need a mason jar with a lid, a carrier oil, and essential oils. Vitamin E oil can also be added to many blends as a stabilizer and preservative. If you do not have all the essential oils for a particular remedy, you can substitute herbs. When making oil blends with essential herbs and oils, additional supplies you will need include a scale, herbs, a grinder, and cheesecloth.

As before, when you are making your essential oils, use ⅛ cup (30 ml) of carrier oil to 10 drops of essential oil. When adding herbs, use ½ cup (120 ml) of carrier oil instead of the ⅛ cup. The additional oil is there to absorb the scent and natural oils of the dried herbs.

Making oil blends is fairly simple. Start by cleaning your mason jar inside and out. If using, put the weighed and ground herbal ingredients into the jar. Add half the carrier oil. Next, add the essential oils. Add the remaining carrier oil. Cover the jar with a lid, shake the jar vigorously, and place it in a cool, dark place. Shake the jar twice daily. After four weeks, strain a small portion of the oil into a small glass to test the scent. If it has the aroma you were trying for, transfer the strained test oil into a new mason jar, and then strain the rest of the oil into the new jar. If it's not as strong as you would like, return the strained portion of the oil to the original jar. Add a few more drops of each essential oil. Shake twice daily. Wait two more weeks, and repeat the strain test.

HEALTH AND WELLNESS
AROMATHERAPY RECIPES

Individual essential oils are powerful tools in health and wellness, but blends of essential oils are much more effective because they combine the benefits of multiple ingredients. The more you work with oils, the more you will find that you have favorite scents and oils that you use more than others. The following simple recipes are some of our favorites that focus on easy-to-obtain herbs and oils that can be found at your local supermarket, health store, or pharmacy. Try a few of these recipes; with a little practice, you will soon be able to create your own blends.

Stress and Anxiety Relief

Anxiety Relief

  5 drops chamomile oil
  5 drops lemongrass oil
  ⅛ cup (30 ml) carrier oil

Stress Relief

  5 drops peppermint oil
  5 drops lavender oil
  ⅛ cup (30 ml) carrier oil

Muscle Tension and Muscle Pain Relief

Muscle-Tension Relief

  ½ tablespoon ground allspice
  ½ tablespoon ground nutmeg
  5 drops geranium oil
  ½ cup (120 ml) carrier oil

Muscle-Pain Relief

  ½ teaspoon cayenne pepper
  ½ teaspoon ground tumeric
  5 drops rose oil
  5 drops tea tree oil
  ½ cup (120 ml) carrier oil

Chest Congestion and Mucus Relief

Chest-Congestion Relief

  5 drops eucalyptus oil
  5 drops pine oil
  ⅛ cup (30 ml) carrier oil

Mucus Buster

  ⅛ cup (5 g) dried nettle leaves
  5 drops frankincense oil
  2 cups (480 ml) carrier oil

Strengthening the Mind

Focus and Concentration

- ½ tablespoon ground myrrh
- 5 drops rosemary oil
- 2 cups (480 ml) carrier oil

Mental Strength and Clarity

- 1 tablespoon dried rosemary
- 5 drops peppermint oil
- 5 drops spearmint oil
- 2 cups (480 ml) carrier oil

Fatigue

Energizer

- ½ tablespoon dried juniper berries
- 5 drops thyme oil
- 2 cups (480 ml) carrier oil

Citrus Energy

- 5 drops lemon oil
- 5 drops lime oil
- ⅛ cup (30 ml) carrier oil

Good Night's Sleep

- 5 drops lemon balm oil
- 5 drops ylang-ylang oil
- ⅛ cup (30 ml) carrier oil

Upset Stomach Relief

Digestion Relief

- ½ tablespoon dried catnip
- 5 drops ginger oil
- 5 drops spearmint oil
- 2 cups (480 ml) carrier oil

THE SPIRITUAL COMPONENT

Aromatherapy can heal not only the body and mind but also the spirit, and it can be a powerful ally in magickal practice as well. The scent of the herbs and oils together triggers changes deep within us, on the spiritual level. This is tremendously powerful and can be a catalyst for change.

In magick, just as in healing, herbs and oils have multiple properties and associations. Some herbs are stronger magickally than others. Magick is very personal, and what works for one person may not work for another. By developing your skills and knowledge about herbs and other plants, you will discover the ones that resonate best and are most compatible with you.

Magickal oils may not have the most pleasant scents, which is fine! The magick in the oils resonates from the energetic properties of the herbs. When you are blending oils, incenses, and baths for magickal and spiritual work, let your intuition guide you. If a particular herb seems to make more sense in a blend than the one you "think" should be included, use it. Your personal guidance and the plant's spirit are talking to you. Listen!

MAGICK BY ESSENTIAL OILS

Essential oils can be used individually in spells or rituals. In casting a love spell, you could anoint yourself with rose or patchouli oil to attract love and bring sensual energy to the situation. If you are having a hard time meditating, you could apply a few drops of frankincense or myrrh oil to your forehead and temples. If you are trying to attract money, a bit of basil oil on a green candle could do the trick. The following list provides several common essential oils and the attributes and areas that they correspond to when used in spells.

ALLSPICE Money and wealth, luck, business success, health

BAY LEAF Psychic awareness, purification

BASIL Happiness, peace, money, aid in meditation and trance work

BLACK PEPPER Mental alertness, protection, physical energy, courage, exorcism

CATNIP Peace, beauty, happiness

CHAMOMILE Sleep, dreams, meditation, peace, money

CINNAMON Physical energy, psychic awareness, prosperity

CLOVE Healing, memory, protection, courage

EUCALYPTUS Health, purification

FRANKINCENSE Spirituality, meditation

GERANIUM Happiness, protection

GINGER Magickal energy, igniting sexual passion, love, money, courage

JUNIPER BERRIES Purification, protection, healing

LAVENDER Health, love, celibacy, conscious mind

LEMON Health, purification

LEMONGRASS Psychic awareness, purification

LEMON BALM Peace, money, purification

LIME Purification, protection

MARIGOLD Health, psychic dreams, comfort, financial security and success

MUGWORT Psychic awareness, psychic dreams, astral projection, spirituality

MYRRH Spirituality, meditation, healing

NUTMEG Magickal energy, psychic awareness, money

PATCHOULI Igniting sexual passion, love, fertility, money, jinx breaking

PEPPERMINT Aid in meditation and trance work, purification, focus

PINE Healing, protection, purification, money

ROSE Igniting sexual passion, love, romance, peace, beauty

ROSEMARY Longevity, memory, love, aid in meditation and trance work

SANDALWOOD Spirituality, meditation, igniting sexual passion, healing

SPEARMINT Healing, protection during sleep, strength of mind

TEA TREE Strength; cleansing; wards off unwanted spiritual attention, negativity, hexes, and curses; healing; protection

THYME Courage, aid in meditation and trance work, health

YLANG-YLANG Peace, igniting sexual passion, love

MAKING MAGICKAL OILS
BOTTLED SPELLS

While individual essential oils are powerful on their own, mixtures allow us to create even more effective oils for spells and rituals. For example, a money oil might include a mix of oil and herbs related to different aspects of money: one oil for attracting money, another oil for financial stability, and a third oil or herb to speed up the process of obtaining money. An oil for love can include oils for romance, lust, attraction, and sexual stimulation.

Magickal oils are essentially spells in a bottle, charged and ready to release their magickal energy upon use. Working with these oils in spells is simple. One way is to wear the oil as a perfume, anointing your body with the magick. In spells that involve candles, you can anoint the candles with an appropriate oil to enhance the spell. All you need to make magick with magickal oils is the oil and your imagination.

Love oils can be used for spells dealing with sexuality, drawing love to you, sparking romance, and growing friendship. Protection oils might be for individual protection, home protection, or business protection. Cleansing oils can help remove negativity hexes or curses, and some remove spiritual blocks. In psychic and spiritual development, the oils would be applied during meditation and ritual work to enhance the spirit and focus the mind. Healing oils send energy toward a person who needs to be healed.

When you start making magickal oils, you will be using a very similar process to that used for health and wellness aromatherapy oils. The major difference is that you are infusing the oils with magick.

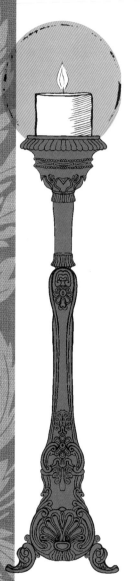

This is done through adding physical, spiritual, mental, and magickal energy during the shaking process.

When you make the magickal oils, the physical action of shaking adds your physical energy into the mix. As you shake the oils, focus on the intent or purpose for each oil. This focus adds mental energy to the blend.

Additional mental, spiritual, and magickal energy is added through the process of colored light visualization. Different colors are used for different purposes, such as blue for healing, green for money, purple for psychic work, and black for protection. To "add" the colored light, you simply envision the colored light filling the oil as you shake the bottle.

The last component to charging magickal oil is the addition of prayers and mantras, which are recited while shaking the oil. A healing oil would use a prayer like "Health and wellness come to me," while a money oil may use words like "Money flowing free, there shall be prosperity." These mantras and prayers are what connect you to the spirit of the plants and activate them for magickal work.

Money

Stressing over money can cause insomnia, digestive issues, anxiety, and fatigue. The following oils are designed to help deal with money stress by drawing in money and protecting financial assets.

Money Draw

- ½ tablespoon ground allspice
- ½ tablespoon ground cinnamon
- 5 drops basil oil
- 5 drops lemon balm oil
- 2 cups (480 ml) carrier oil

Protect Money

- 2 teaspoons dried marigold
- 5 drops nutmeg oil
- 2 cups (480 ml) carrier oil

Love

Love comes in many forms, from romantic, sexual, and passionate to parental, familial, and even friendly. No matter the type of love you are looking for, these oils can attract the right kind into your life.

Simple Love

- 5 drops rose oil
- 5 drops lavender oil
- ½ cup (120 ml) carrier oil

Ignite My Passion

- 5 drops ginger oil
- 5 drops patchouli oil
- 5 drops ylang-ylang oil
- 1½ cups (360 ml) carrier oil

Protection

Protection magick deals with creating a sense of safety. In some cases, protection requires gaining the courage and strength to stand up and defend yourself. Other protection spells deal with keeping negativity away.

Stand and Fight

- 1 tablespoon ground black pepper
- 5 drops clove oil
- $^3/_4$ cup (180 ml) carrier oil

House Protection

- 5 drops thyme oil
- 5 drops geranium oil
- 5 drops tea tree oil
- $^1/_4$ cup (60 ml) cups carrier oil

Cleansing and Purification

Over time, all our thoughts, both positive and negative—as well as actions taken or not taken—build up an energetic residue. Cleansing and purification oils help remove that psychic buildup, allowing only the energies that serve you best to remain.

Citrus Cleansing

- 10 drops lemon oil
- 5 drops lime oil
- $^1/_4$ cup (60 ml) carrier oil

Purification

- 5 drops juniper oil
- 5 drops pine oil
- 5 drops eucalyptus oil
- $1^1/_2$ (360 ml) cups carrier oil

Meditation, Psychic Abilities, and Mental Focus

In witchcraft, there are some spells and rituals that help develop psychic gifts and abilities. These gifts can involve clairvoyance (psychic sight), mediumship, divination (the ability to read tarot cards, runes, and other such tools), aura reading and healing, and much more. Developing these skills can help you become more in tune with yourself and your spirit through the development of your intuition. The following oils help with meditation, mental clarity, and connecting to yourself spiritually.

Spirituality

- 5 drops frankincense oil
- 5 drops myrrh oil
- ¼ cups (60 ml) carrier oil

Meditation

- 1 tablespoon dried catnip
- 5 drops chamomile oil
- 5 drops sandalwood oil
- ¾ cup (180 ml) carrier oil

Psychic Awareness

- 2 teaspoons dried marigold
- 5 whole dried bay leaves
- 5 drops lemongrass oil
- ¾ cup (180 ml) carrier oil

AROMATHERAPY BATH SALTS

Baths are powerful tools that can be used for health and wellness. Sometimes when we have sore muscles, suffer from chest congestion, or feel stressed, depressed, or anxious—or even unable to sleep—a soak in a hot bath can be all the medicine we need. Aromatherapy baths with bath salts combine the natural relief that comes from hot water with the power of essential oils to provide a soothing, sensational bath that rejuvenates the mind, body, and spirit.

An aromatherapy bath works in two ways. First, there is the hot water itself, which relaxes and releases muscle tension naturally. Second, the heat from the water also allows the salts to dissolve more easily so they can release their calming, aromatherapeutic scents into the bathwater.

Crafting Bath Salts

When it comes to supplies for making bath salts, very little equipment is needed. Most of the necessary items can be bought at your local supermarket or department store. The materials needed are: a scale, a grinder or blender, a mixing bowl, measuring cups, a mason jar for storage, essential oils, herbs, a mixing spoon, and Epsom salts. You should store all of these items together in a specific place reserved just for ingredients used in making bath salts.

Crafting bath salts is very simple. To start, weigh and grind your dried herbs. Once ground, pour them into the mixing bowl. Take the mixing spoon and stir the herbs well. For each ounce of herbs, add 4 ounces (110 g) of Epsom salts to the bowl. While adding the Epsom salts, stir the mix frequently. The last step is to add each essential oil one at a time. Stir the mixture frequently. Once all of the essential oils have been mixed in, pour the completed bath salts into a mason jar. Label the jar. The bath salts are now ready for use.

Anxiety and Stress Relief

Anxiety Relief

5 drops ylang-ylang oil
5 drops lemon balm oil
4 ounces (110 g) Epsom salts

Stress Relief

2 tablespoons dried spearmint
5 drops lavender oil
4 ounces (110 g) Epsom salts

Muscle Pain and Muscle Tension Relief

Pain Relief

1 tablespoon ground cinnamon

1 tablespoon ground clove

5 drops tea tree oil

4 ounces (110 g) Epsom salts

Tension Relief

1 tablespoon ground allspice

1 tablespoon ground nutmeg

5 drops geranium oil

4 ounces (110 g) Epsom salts

Chest Congestion and Upset Stomach Relief

Chest Congestion Relief

5 drops eucalyptus oil

5 drops pine oil

4 ounces (110 g) Epsom salts

Improve Digestion

1 tablespoon ground ginger

1 tablespoon dried thyme

5 drops frankincense oil

4 ounces (110 g) Epsom salts

Fatigue

Fatigue Relief

2 tablespoons dried rosemary

5 drops lemon oil

5 drops juniper oil

4 ounces (110 g) Epsom salts

Sleep Assistance

5 drops chamomile oil

5 drops peppermint oil

4 ounces (110 g) Epsom salts

Depression Relief and Mood Elevation

Happiness

- 2 tablespoons dried catnip
- 5 drops rose oil
- 4 ounces (110 g) Epsom salts

Mood Elevator

- 2 tablespoons dried basil
- 5 drops lemongrass oil
- 4 ounces (110 g) Epsom salts

Mood Stabilizer

- 5 drops lime oil
- 5 drops myrrh oil
- 4 ounces (110 g) Epsom salts

Once you have your bath salts prepared, it's time to take a relaxing bath. Fill the tub with hot water. Make sure the water is as hot as you can stand. When the tub is about a quarter full, sprinkle 3 teaspoons of the bath salts into the tub. Using your hands, stir the bathwater, mixing the salt into the water. When the tub is full, step in and soak. As you soak, let your body and mind relax. Remain in the tub for thirty minutes. Dry off with a towel.

THE POWER OF RITUAL BATHS

In witchcraft, oftentimes the only ritual baths we think of are baths taken prior to sabbats (seasonal festivals relating to solstices and equinoxes) to cleanse our minds, bodies, and spirits prior to the ritual, but ritualized baths provide many avenues for working magick. Conjure or hoodoo (traditional African American folk magick) also uses ritual baths for cleansing and blessings. A hoodoo worker may prescribe a ritual bath for a client to open up prosperity or to remove a hex or a curse (known as "uncrossing"). Other folk magick traditions include washing one's home or business for success, protection, and blessings.

The primary difference in preparation between ritual baths and aromatherapy baths is the addition of prayer. Ritual baths are prepared with prayers (like the Psalms or runic chants , or any personal prayer or petition you wish) recited over them. These prayers and chants empower the baths with the essence of spirit as well as activate the spiritual essences within the herbs and oils.

Unlike aromatherapy baths, ritual baths do not require a full soak. In fact, you don't even need a tub to soak in. Long ago when not everyone had a tub or running water, ritual baths were often done in washbasins used for laundry or dishes. You would sit or stand in the basin and pour the bath mixture over your body from head to toe. Today, if you have a tub, you can do a full-immersion soak. If you do not have a tub, you can simply sit or stand in your shower stall. Take a wash basin containing water and bath salts, and pour it over you from top to bottom to *remove* something, or splash from your feet to your crown to *bring* something to you.

If you are washing a house or a workplace/space, take a washbasin throughout the area as you wipe down all surfaces. When cleansing objects, placing them in the bowl or washbasin is fine. When washing yourself or others, a sponge bath is all that is needed. The important thing is contact with the herbs and the water.

Love and Sexuality

These baths are designed to open you up to opportunities for love and sexual intimacy.

Spice Up Desire

- 5 drops ginger oil
- 5 drops sandalwood oil
- 1 tablespoon dried patchouli leaves
- 4 ounces (110 g) Epsom salts

Soft-and-Sweet Love

- 1 tablespoon dried rose petals
- 1 tablespoon dried rosemary
- 4 ounces (110 g) Epsom salts

Happiness

- 1 tablespoon dried catnip
- 1 tablespoon dried basil
- 5 drops geranium oil
- 4 ounces (110 g) Epsom salts

Money and Success

These baths are designed to increase luck, bring success, and open any blocks in your path to financial stability.

Luck and Success

- 1 tablespoon ground allspice
- 5 drops chamomile oil
- 4 ounces (110 g) Epsom salts

Money

- 1 tablespoon ground allspice
- 1 tablespoon ground ginger
- 5 drops patchouli oil
- 4 ounces (110 g) Epsom salts

Meditation, Psychic Awareness, and Spirituality

These baths are designed to help relax an individual, allowing them to be more in tune with their psychic abilities.

Meditation

- 1 tablespoon dried lavender
- 5 drops myrrh oil
- 5 drops ylang-ylang oil
- 4 ounces (110 g) Epsom salts

Enhance My Spirit

- 1 tablespoon dried mugwort
- 5 drops frankincense oil
- 5 drops myrrh oil
- 5 drops sandalwood oil
- 4 ounces (110 g) Epsom salts

Psychic Awareness

- 1 tablespoon ground nutmeg
- 1 tablespoon dried thyme
- 5 drops cinnamon oil
- 5 drops marigold oil
- 4 ounces Epsom salts

Protection and Courage

These baths are designed to encourage you to have the strength to stand up for yourself and to ward against evil or ill wishes.

Defenders

- 1 tablespoon ground clove
- 1 tablespoon dried juniper berries
- 5 drops lime oil
- 4 ounces (110 g) Epsom salts

Warding Against Evil

- 5 drops pine oil
- 5 drops tea tree oil
- 4 ounces (110 g) Epsom salts

Cleanse and Banish

These baths are designed to spiritually cleanse and banish anything that causes you issues.

Negativity Be Banished

- 1 tablespoon ground black pepper
- 5 whole dried bay leaves
- 5 drops lemongrass oil
- 4 ounces (110 g) Epsom salts

Purify and Cleanse the Spirit

- 1 tablespoon dried peppermint
- 1 tablespoon dried spearmint
- 5 drops lemon oil
- 5 drops lemon balm oil
- 4 ounces (110 g) Epsom salts

Aromatherapy helps you reconnect with Mother Earth. May these oils and baths supercharge your life with health and wellness as you travel on your spiritual journey.

Chapter 3

Crystal
Power

**THE
HIDDEN WISDOM
OF GEMS**

Stones and crystals with powerful healing attributes can be found almost anywhere here on Earth. From beach pebbles to rocks found in the woods and in streams, you can walk almost anywhere and find a stone that has quartz or another crystalline mineral within it. These stones are as much a part of the magickal and healing world as herbs and flowers are, yet most of the time we see them as things of beauty or items to use for jewelry. Often we do not think about how stones like hematite can help with anxiety, or how bloodstone can be used to cleanse the blood. Just like herbs, a wonderful world of healing and healthful properties exist within crystals and gems. It's time to bring some of that magick out from the depths of the earth and into the light of day. When we work with these elements for health and wellness, we are drawing on energy from the very beginning of time.

COLOR YOUR LIFE BEAUTIFUL WITH CRYSTALS

When it comes to crystals, we are attracted to them partly for their colors and the way we react to those colors. In spiritual work, colors have a very rich history of use—blue is common for healing, and red is universal for love and passion. The colors that a crystal emanates give you an insight into how you can work with it magickally. Here is a simple list of color associations:

WHITE Pure spirit, innocence, blank slate (any purpose)

RED Love, life, sex, romance, power, element of fire

ORANGE Success, memory, gaining energy

GREEN Money, fertility, success, growth, life-earth element

BLUE Healing, peace, dream work

GOLD Money, success, Sun God

YELLOW Success, luck, element of air

SILVER Intuition, money, psychic ability, Moon Goddess

PURPLE Intuition, psychic energy, mental focus, spirituality

BLACK Protection, grounding, strength

Now that we have gone through color associations, let us look at some crystals and their magickal associations:

AMETHYST Dreams, healing, psychic ability, peace, love, protection against thieves, courage, happiness

AVENTURINE Mental focus and psychic ability, eyesight, gambling and general luck, money, peace, healing

BLOODSTONE Healing, victory, courage, success in legal matters and business, wealth

CARNELIAN Peace, relief from depression

CITRINE Success, protection, anti-nightmare, psychic ability

CLEAR QUARTZ Boosts any other crystals or herbs, spirituality, protection, healing, psychic ability, power

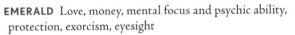

DIAMOND Spirituality, reconciliation, help with sexual dysfunction, protection, courage, peace, love, healing, strength

EMERALD Love, money, mental focus and psychic ability, protection, exorcism, eyesight

FLUORITE Mental focus and psychic ability

GARNET Healing, protection, strength

HEMATITE Grounding, healing, divination

IRON PYRITE (Fool's Gold) Money, divination, luck

JADEITE Love, healing, longevity, wisdom, protection, prosperity, money

JET Protection, anti-nightmare, luck, divination, health

LABRADORITE Peace of mind, peace, happiness, tranquility, relaxation

LAPIS LAZULI Healing, joy, love, fidelity, psychic ability, protection, courage

MALACHITE Power, protection, love, peace, business success

MOONSTONE Love, divination, psychic ability, gardening, youth, protection, dieting, Moon Goddess

MOSS AGATE Gardening, riches, happiness, long life, fertility

RED JASPER Protection against poison and negativity, curing fevers, healing, beauty, grace

ROSE QUARTZ Love, open-heart chakra, peace, happiness

RUBY Wealth, protection, power, joy, anti-nightmare

SMOKY QUARTZ Grounding, relief from depression

SUNSTONE Protection, energy, health, sexual energy, Sun God

TIGEREYE Money, prosperity, courage, energy, luck, divination

One of the best ways to work with crystals in magick is to simply carry them in your pocket or place them somewhere hidden but where the energy can still be effective. Ancient warriors carried bloodstones as charms for victory and to help with bleeding injuries during battle. By carrying tigereye in your pocket you can bring an increase in luck and prosperity. If you are starting to feel fatigued, touch the stone and you'll get energized. If you are running a small business, place a small malachite stone and an iron pyrite stone behind the register to attract customers and boost sales. If you place moss agate in your garden, it will be much healthier and more fertile.

Now that the crystals have revealed their magick to us, it is time to move further down the road of health and wellness.

May the crystal light guide you into health and wellness.

CRYSTALS ARE YOUR BEST FRIENDS

There is a large variety of healing crystals on the market. Many of them are handled by hundreds of people during the journey from the earth to your hands. This is one of the reasons it can be hard to find a crystal's unique energy when you first handle it. Before you purchase crystals, there is a simple and effective meditation you can do to find and connect with the crystal that most aligns with your spirit.

Crystal Alignment Meditation
SIMPLE TRICKS TO SOOTHE YOUR SOUL

When standing before the crystals, close your eyes and focus on the moment. Take three slow breaths: inhale to the count of four, hold for a count of four, exhale for a count of four, and then hold for another four counts. Now state firmly in your mind: "My spirit vibrates in harmony with (insert crystal type here)." Keep mentally reciting that chant until you feel an energetic shift in yourself. Now open your eyes and start to feel the crystals before you. Hold them and touch them. The crystal that is right for you will feel like it's humming in your hand. This sensation is the alignment of your energy and the crystal energy.

Boosting Your Crystal Power

Simple Cleansing Ritual

Before you begin to work with the crystals, you need to cleanse them. This cleansing is both physical and energetic. It will remove any dust or dirt that may have accumulated over time. The more important reason for the cleansing, however, is to remove the energy of anyone else who has handled them, allowing only your energy and the crystal's energy to remain.

Materials

> Your crystals
>
> Bowl of soapy water
>
> Sea salt (in a small bowl)
>
> Bowl of cold water

Ritual

Take all your crystals and place them in the bowl of soapy water. Use your hands to rub the crystals clean in the soapy water. As you wash them, see that all the energy of others is removed and that only your energy remains. As you wash them, chant:

> *"Water, cleanse and clean.*
> *Remove the negative unseen."*

When they feel lighter, individually place them in the bowl of salt. The salt will ground them in your energy and their energy, and remove any remaining energy.

Next, dip them in the bowl of cold water to rinse off the salt but keep the energetic process. As you remove them from the water, state:

"By the water, no more negativity.
By the water, blessed be."

Your crystals are now blessed and cleansed. They are ready to be used.

CRYSTAL PROPERTIES
LOOKING INTO THE CRYSTAL BALL

Now that you have aligned yourself with the crystals, purchased them, cleansed them, and blessed them, it's time to start working with them. The following crystals can be used in single charms or in the complex elixirs discussed on pages 82–83.

AMETHYST Relieves arthritis, asthma, anxiety, fatigue, insomnia, and stress; improves circulation

AMBER Relieves asthma, constipation, and headaches; boosts energy

AVENTURINE Relieves anxiety and fatigue, boosts immunity

BLOODSTONE Improves circulation, relieves fatigue, boosts immunity

CARNELIAN Relieves arthritis and fatigue, improves circulation, aids concentration, aids fertility, boosts energy

CITRINE Relieves constipation, improves digestion

CLEAR QUARTZ Aids concentration; boosts energy, immunity, and the properties and strength of all other crystals

DIAMOND Relieves anxiety and depression, purifies, cleanses, regulates hormones

EMERALD Relieves asthma, detoxifies, cleanses, boosts immunity, relieves headaches

FLUORITE Relieves arthritis, aids concentration (*note: do not use in an elixir or crystal water*)

GARNET Relieves arthritis and depression, improves circulation, aids fertility

HEMATITE Relieves anxiety, arthritis, headaches, and insomnia; improves circulation; aids sleep

IRON PYRITE (Fool's Gold) Relieves asthma, improves digestion

JADEITE Relieves depression, balances the nervous system

JET Relieves headaches and depression

LABRADORITE Improves digestion, relieves stress

LAPIS LAZULI Relieves depression, headaches, insomnia, and stress; boosts immunity

MALACHITE Relieves asthma, boosts immunity (*note: do not use in an elixir or crystal water*)

MOONSTONE Relieves anxiety, aids fertility

MOSS AGATE Relieves depression, boosts immunity

RED JASPER Improves circulation, aids concentration, relieves constipation

ROSE QUARTZ Relieves anxiety, headaches, and stress; aids fertility

RUBY Improves circulation, relieves constipation

SMOKY QUARTZ Relieves anxiety, stress, and headaches

SUNSTONE Relieves depression and fatigue

TIGEREYE Relieves anxiety, asthma, and depression

Crystal Charms

Humans have been working with crystals in the form of charms for as long as they have been able to dig crystals out of the earth and recognize the deep healing potential of the planet. Just like with herbs, there are many different ways we can work with crystals for healing. Most commonly, people create little charms, or talismans, so that they can carry the stones with them at all times. The stones and crystals used in such charms have been referred to as the "bones of the earth," as their power comes from the very core of the earth. Such charms allow us to connect to the deep, supportive power of the earth.

Charms often come in the form of jewelry, such as bracelets or earrings. Jewelry charms are very popular, as they can be worn in one location (such as on the wrist, earlobe, or finger) but have an effect on the entire body. This is because the energetic properties of crystals that allow them to work for health and wellness connect the mind, the body, and the spirit all at once.

Jewelry is also an inconspicuous way to work with a variety of gems and crystals. It is something that you can wear every day or on special occasions as needed. You simply touch the jewelry while you are wearing it to active the charm. Items like hematite bracelets for grounding (relieving anxiety) are quite common.

The most popular crystal charm combination is hematite, amethyst, and clear quartz. When you look at the combined health and wellness properties of these three stones, it's no wonder. They are often grouped together because they aid in similar ailments, such as anxiety, stress relief, and poor circulation. Hematite adds in the ability to deal with headaches, while amethyst adds relief for breathing issues. Clear quartz supports the properties of all other crystals, and it is an immune booster. By combining it with hematite and amethyst, you have a perfect overall-health-and-wellness charm.

Bloodstone can be carried on a chain that dangles above the heart chakra. This position activates the charm, allowing the energy to be dispersed throughout the body as needed. When centered over the heart, this stone helps circulation. When the wearer holds the charm, they can boost their immune system and gain relief from fatigue.

Everything on Earth has energy. With crystals, we often don't think of using that energy in a form other than as a physical charm, but there are many different forms of working with crystals for their purely energetic properties, such as crystal waters, elixirs, and essences. Many of these are relatively new methods that deal with crystal energy in a nontraditional way.bath.

Crystal Essences

AN INTERVIEW WITH CHARISSA ISKIWITCH

With the rise in popularity of crystal elixirs and crystal healing, many shops are starting to offer different types of crystal-healing products. Charissa Iskiwitch, founder of the Silver Pine Grove coven in Georgia and owner of Charissa's Cauldron website, is an expert in crystal essences, which are infusions of water and alcohol (as a preservative) made with plants or crystals. Essences carry the energetic properties of the substances they are made with, and they are ideal for addressing the emotional and mental aspects of health and well-being.

The most well-known essences are probably the Bach flower remedies, which were developed by British homeopathic doctor Edward Bach in the 1930s.

Essences can be taken orally or administered through a mist sprayer, in a cream, or in a bath. When taken orally, the standard dosage is 4 drops 4 times daily, but, as always, consult with your health-care practitioner before using. It is important to remember that you are not actually taking in any of the physical crystals—just the energetic properties of them.

The following interview of Charissa was conducted for her insight on working with crystal healing and crystal essences.

How long have you been working with crystals for health and healing?

I have always been drawn to stones. Even as a child, when helping my grandmother in the garden, I would set aside rocks we dug up into a pile to clean and play with. Later, in high school, I ran across a book in the library (one of my favorite places) about ancient Egypt and was fascinated by the references to their use of crystals in healing.

That started me on a quest. When I later learned energy-healing modalities such as Reiki, I naturally incorporated crystals into that work. I use crystals in healing, spell work, and basically all of my practices.

Why (did you create) a line of crystal essences? Herbs and flowers are known to have healing properties, but crystals . . . not so much.

I suppose because I started reading and studying about the healing properties of crystals in my teen years, it never occurred to me that this information is anything but widely known. Crystals have been used for thousands of years in healing by many cultures.

Do you have a favorite crystal essence, and why?

I would have to say hematite. I use that regularly to help keep me grounded and on task. I keep the stones spread around the house to absorb negative energy. I carry one in my pocket on days when I feel particularly stressed. I find that it goes well in any blend I make to help keep me grounded and free of negativity.

If you could list three crystals that are must-haves for health, wellness, and connection to the spirit, what would they be?

I recommend rose quartz, hematite, and amethyst. Both amethyst and hematite can be used for protection. Both rose quartz and amethyst are good for emotional well-being. Much of our health can be affected by our emotional well-being.

What advice would you give to someone who wanted to make their own essences?

Be aware of the physical properties of the plant or crystal you are using. If there is a chance of allergic reaction, or if the crystal has metallic properties, err on the side of caution and use the No-Touch Method of making your essences [see page 81]. In the case of essences, you want to make sure you go through the entire dilution process. Make the mother bottle [see page 80]. Then make the stock bottle. From the stock bottle, you would make the dosage bottles. That will dilute the formulas substantially.

Aside from your crystal essences, do you think there are other ways you can work with crystals for healing?

Absolutely! I use crystals when doing energy healing, like Reiki. I use them for clearing chakras. When I'm searching for answers, I will sometimes choose a stone to help clarify my dreams and sleep with it under my pillow.

CRYSTAL WATER
DRINK YOUR WAY TO BETTER HEALTH

It is important to understand that with crystal water—like with the crystal essences mentioned previously—there is no actual physical substance from the crystals in the water after the preparation is complete. It is only the energy of the crystals that is transferred. Crystal waters are energetic healing waters. The crystal is used only during the preparation to create energized water. Once the water is created, the crystal is removed, and the water is strained and bottled.

In order to make the best crystal waters, you need filtered water. You can use tap water that has been filtered, unless you are in a city (city water is often treated with chlorine), in which case you should use distilled or bottled water. You need a glass bottle or jar to make the original batch in and another glass container in which to store the completed remedy. Last but not least, you need to have the appropriate selection of crystals for your remedy.

You can use a single crystal water to get the effects of an individual crystal, or you can make blends to suit specific needs. The process is the same for both types of water and is fairly simple. Place the crystals in the bottom of the glass container you are using to make your original, or "mother," batch. Add enough water to fill the container, and place the container outside in the sun or on a sunny windowsill. Let the crystal water sit in the sun for two to eight hours. Once it has been steeped in the sunlight, remove the crystal and strain the charged water into your other glass container using cheesecloth. The remedy is now ready to be used.

Dosages of crystal-water remedies should be about 2–3 drops in a glass of water or juice 3–4 times a day. This allows the energetic properties of the crystals to be slowly and evenly distributed throughout your body as the day goes on.

No-Touch Method

There are some crystal elixirs and waters that need to be produced via the no-touch method. Some crystals and minerals—including malachite, azurite, fluorite, jet, sulfur, serpentine, tigereye, tiger iron, and turquoise—have metallic elements, such as iron, or other components that can be absorbed into the water but should not touch your skin and that you should not drink. If you are unsure of a crystal or its components, you should use this no-touch method.

You will need a small bowl, a large bowl, your crystal or crystals, water, and a bottle or jar. Make sure that the larger bowl is big enough so that the smaller bowl can nest within it nicely while leaving room for water.

Place the crystal or crystals in the smaller bowl. Place the smaller bowl within the larger bowl. Fill the larger bowl with enough water that the water level is above the height of the crystal(s) in the smaller bowl. Once you have reached that level, place the bowls outside in the sun or on a sunny windowsill for two to eight hours. Then bottle the water from the larger bowl and use as needed in the same dosage as regular crystal waters.

Quick and Easy Crystal-Water Recipes

Here are some simple crystal-water remedies using crystals that are easily obtained online or at your many metaphysical, jewelry-making, or even craft stores. You only need one stone of each crystal to make these remedies. One of the great things about using crystals for healing is that they are reusable. So if you only have one amethyst stone, say, you can make one remedy with it, cleanse it, and use it in another remedy. It's a great way to get multiple uses out of one item. Just remember to cleanse your crystals between uses.

Anxiety Relief

Amethyst
Rose quartz
Moonstone

Arthritis Relief

Carnelian
Garnet
Hematite

Asthma Relief*

Amethyst
Iron pyrite
Tigereye

Constipation Relief

Citrine
Red jasper

Depression Relief

Garnet
Jadeite
Lapis lazuli
Sunstone
Moss agate

---

* Use the No-Touch Method described on page 81.

Digestive Relief *

Citrine
Iron pyrite
Labradorite
Energy Boost
Carnelian
Clear quartz

Fatigue Relief

Aventurine
Carnelian
Sunstone

Fertility

Carnelian
Garnet
Moonstone
Rose quartz

Headache Relief

Clear quartz
Hematite
Lapis lazuli
Rose quartz

Immunity Boost

Aventurine
Bloodstone
Clear quartz
Lapis lazuli

Improve Circulation

Bloodstone
Hematite

Improve Concentration

Carnelian
Clear quartz
Red jasper

Insomnia Relief

Amethyst
Hematite
Lapis lazuli

Stress Relief

Lapis lazuli
Smoky quartz
Rose quartz

* Use the No-Touch Method described on page 81.

CHAKRA BALANCING

Chakra balancing is one of the most common uses of crystal healing. The word *chakra* means "wheel" or "turning" in ancient Sanskrit, and yogic Hindu and Tantric Buddhist traditions describe chakras as energetic centers, or energy wheels, in the human body. There are seven main chakras, from the top of your head to the base of your spine, and each one is associated with a specific area of the physical body as well as with a spiritual attribute. When a chakra becomes blocked or unbalanced, there can be issues of physical health as well as spiritual health.

By balancing the chakras, a person can become more relaxed. It is a treatment for the mind, body, and spirit that helps a person become more in tune with their complete self. This reduces stress and anxiety, increases productivity, and can even help cure depression. Some chakra imbalances can also cause physical ailments like colds, flus, and digestive issues.

The following list provides general locations of the chakras and what systems in the body they relate to, as well as symptoms of a blocked chakra.

✳ Root Chakra

LOCATION Base of the spine

MIND/BODY SYSTEMS Survival instinct, sexual glands, cleansing/purging the body, relationship with self

BLOCKS CAN CAUSE Sexual dysfunction, lack of enjoyment in life, depression, feeling ungrounded

✳ Sacral Chakra

LOCATION Naval/belly

MIND/BODY SYSTEMS Kidneys, intestines, lower digestive system, spleen, pancreas, relationships with others

BLOCKS CAN CAUSE Ulcers, mood swings, digestive issues, inability to communicate with others, inability to trust one's instincts

✳ Solar Plexus Chakra

LOCATION Right below the diaphragm muscle

MIND/BODY SYSTEMS Metabolism, stomach, liver, gall bladder, adrenal glands, muscular system, sense of power and will

BLOCKS CAN CAUSE Power control, addiction, emotional instability, imbalances in the liver, gall bladder, or adrenal glands

✳ Heart Chakra

LOCATION Sternum

MIND/BODY SYSTEMS Heart, circulatory system, skin, immune system, thymus gland, bridge between highest and lowest selves, brings unconditional and divine love

BLOCKS CAN CAUSE Circulatory disorders, lowered immune responses (getting sick more frequently), inability to form loving relationships, inability to express emotions, inability to trust others, sense of shame

ஃ Throat Chakra

LOCATION Vocal chords/voice box

MIND/BODY SYSTEMS Respiratory system, larynx, tonsils, thyroid, expressions of thoughts and emotions, spiritual and psychic hearing

BLOCKS CAN BE CAUSE Panic attacks, hyperventilation, asthma attacks, overactivity, lethargy, communication issues

ஃ Third Eye Chakra

LOCATION Slightly above and between the eyes (center of the forehead)

MIND/BODY SYSTEMS Pineal gland, sight, nervous system, psychic sight, spirit sight

BLOCKS CAN BE CAUSE Nervous disorders, migraine headaches, inability to see the truth about your life

ஃ Crown Chakra

LOCATION Top of the head

MIND/BODY SYSTEMS Pituitary gland, hormones, immune system, higher consciousness, direct spirit connection to the divine

BLOCKS CAN CAUSE Hormonal imbalances, lack of connection to the self, lack of sense of meaning in life, sense of abandonment from the gods and spirits

CHAKRAS AND STONES

One of the ways to treat an imbalance in chakra energy is to use gems and crystals. Every chakra has its own associated colors. This color energy is also found in crystals with corresponding colors. Some crystals are more commonly used than others for chakra work. Now that we have covered what the chakras are and how they interact and work with the body, it's time to learn which stones you can use to correct imbalances and optimize your health.

Root Chakra

Color Red
Stone Red jasper or garnet

Sacral Chakra

Color Orange
Stone Sunstone or carnelian

Solar Plexus Chakra

Color Yellow
Stone Citrine or tigerye

Heart Chakra

Color Green
Stone Aventurine or emerald

Throat Chakra

Color Blue
Stone Lapis lazuli or sapphire

Third Eye Chakra

Color Purple or indigo
Stone Amethyst or charoite

Crown Chakra

Color Purple or white
Stone Clear quartz, opal, or diamond

Chakra Balancing Ritual

This is a simple ritual that you can perform to balance and cleanse your chakras. This ritual is best performed during a waning moon, because you are removing or banishing the energy that is blocking your chakras to clear them for future health and success. For best results, perform the ritual once a month to keep your chakras clear and the energy flowing. It is a good idea to keep the crystals used for this ritual separate from the other crystals you work with. By keeping them separate, each crystal will build up energy related to its specific chakra. This will allow you to create seven powerful individual crystal charms to be used for each chakra as needed.

Materials

    Soft instrumental music

2 blue candles

1 white candle

    Lavender incense (loose or stick)

1 of each of the following stones:
    Garnet
    Carnelian
    Tigereye
    Aventurine
    Lapis lazuli
    Amethyst
    Clear quartz

Ritual

Turn on the music and light the 2 blue candles. As you light the candles, state:

"By the blessings of this light,
Healing comes on this night."

Light the white candle and state:

"By the powers of the sacred light,
Grant to me healing sight."

Light the lavender incense.

Place the crystals on the floor and sit down. (Lotus position is good if it is comfortable for you. If not, any comfortable sitting position on the floor is fine.) Once you are comfortable, take three deep breaths in using the four-count method—count in for four, hold for four, exhale for four, and hold for a count of four again. Close your eyes and focus inward on the base of your spine, around the location of your tailbone. Envision a ball of light rotating at the base of your spine, reaching down into the earth.

Once you feel yourself deep within the earth, watch the ball of light split into two different lines. These are your roots. Now, with each breath in, pull up that energy from the earth through your right root. With each exhale, push all negativity that does not serve you out through your left root. Once you see both roots pulsating with the energy of the earth, you have been grounded, connected, and your roots are set.

Now it is time to align, cleanse, and open your chakras. You are rooted to the earth from head to toe. As you begin to work with the chakras, watch as the negative energy flows down the left root and the invigorating energy to heal and cleanse each chakra comes up from the right root.

From here, you can proceed with the crystal work with your eyes open or closed. It depends on how you visualize best.

Start with the garnet for your Root Chakra. Hold the crystal at the chakra point. Feel it start to pulse and align with the chakra. Visualize and see the chakra as a red ball of light spinning clockwise. Notice if there are any dark spots or if the chakra is spinning slowly. Focus on removing those dark areas. Notice the chakra start to spin brighter and faster as the dark spots are removed. When the spots are removed and the chakra is a clear red and spinning quickly, place the garnet back on the floor and pick up the carnelian stone.

Repeat the visualization you did for the Root Chakra with the Sacral Chakra. This time, the chakra will be orange. When you feel it is spinning with a clear, orange light, place the carnelian stone on the floor and pick up the tigereye.

Continue with the stones and, in order of the chakras, repeat the visualization: tigereye (yellow), aventurine (green), lapis lazuli (blue), amethyst (purple), clear quartz (white).

Once you have all the chakras spinning clean, clear, and bright in a clockwise fashion, hold their image in your mind. Watch the light of the chakras spinning, interacting and filling your whole body with their energy. Feel yourself becoming lighter and balanced. When you can no longer hold the visualization, gently release it knowing that your spirit body has become your physical body.

Place your hands on the floor and focus any excess energy into the earth. See the energy that you do not need entering the earth and being used for plants and animals.

Extinguish the candles and put the crystals away.

If you feel dizzy or light-headed, eat something light, like a peanut-butter sandwich or fruit. This will help ground you and bring you back to day-to-day life. Repeat these four lines three times:

> *"May my body be at one with the universe.*
> *May my mind be at one with the universe.*
> *May my soul be at one with the universe.*
> *May I be whole and one."*

Once you have repeated the prayer, you can conclude with:

> *"So mote it be."*

Part Two

SPIRIT SPELLS
AND
SPIRITUALITY

Chapter 4

Spellcast Your Way to Better Health

RECHARGE YOUR MIND, BODY, AND SPIRIT

Living with magick is an integral part of being a witch. From making potions and brews to casting spells for health and wellness, spellcraft is an essential component to the art of witchery and plays an important role in a witch's daily life. When working with any kind of ritualistic practice, there is a common connection both to the physical world and to the spiritual plane. Magick begins when we are able to tap into the creative force of the universe, which then goes on to implement the changes we require in our lives. From charging an amulet for protection to placing a basil leaf in the cash register of a business—even blessing a fresh pot of chicken noodle soup—this magick can occur every day in the life of a spellcaster. Magick does not have to be complicated. It's actually very simple, and when practiced regularly, it is an effective tool for living a happy, healthy, and holistic life.

Practical Magick
LIVING A MAGICKAL LIFE

Every living thing on the planet, regardless of its physical body, is pure energy and has a spirit. By connecting to these energetic forces, you can work spells for almost any need.

A key part of many spells is visualization. Visualizations create ripples in the universe that bounce back to you and focus your consciousness into doing the right thing. It is best to concentrate on just one thing at a time. If you try to cast too many spells at once, the results are likely to be ineffective—you may have a spell overload, causing you to lose focus.

SPELLS FOR WELL-BEING

In order to function well, it is important to take care not only of your physical self but also of your mental well-being. The spells below will set you in good stead for the day and leave you with an inner peace, a sense of clarity, and the stamina to embrace the moment.

Daily Shower Spell

Materials

> Water
>
> Soap or shower gel
>
> Shampoo and conditioner

Ritual

Start the shower with the water as hot as you can stand it, and step inside. Once inside the shower, let the water run over you from head to toe. As you bathe, watch the water going down the drain and picture it in your mind as a gray color. Next, visualize the water removing all of your anxieties and any issues you had from the day before.

Begin to wash your hair with shampoo. In your mind's eye, see the stress and anxiety leaving your body and entering into the shampoo bubbles.

Repeat the visualization process with the conditioner. Take the soap or shower gel and, starting with your face, wash your whole body several times, cleansing from head to toe. As you lather, say these words over and over:

"Water, water, wash away. Water, water, cleanse today."

Once you are clean, rinse off all of the suds. The lather will absorb your troubles and wash them down the drain. Cool the shower temperature slightly, and bathe for a few more minutes in the refreshing water. When you feel comfortably cleansed and refreshed, step out and dry off with a towel from top to bottom while repeating these words:

"By the earth in the soap,
By the air in the steam,
By the fire which heats the water,
By the water that washes,
I am cleansed, clean, and ready for the day."

Self-Love Spell

Materials

> After-shower body lotion
>
> Any beauty supplies you use regularly, such as skin-care products, makeup, powders, face cream, and shaving gels (for men or women)

Ritual

It is hard for others to love you if you do not love yourself first. Sit on the floor or on your bed in a comfortable position and surround yourself with all of your beauty and skin-care products. Imagine that these products are covered in a pink light. Slowly start to run your hands over your body from your feet to your head. As you connect with your body, start the chant:

"Love within, love without,
I love myself without doubt."

After a while, you will start to feel the pink light become part of your body. At this point, begin to apply the after-shower lotion and repeat the chant. As you smooth the lotion over your skin, visualize the pink light entering you through your pores. When you have covered your body from head to toe, stand up and speak loudly:

"I am loved."

Continue to get ready for the day as you normally would. If at any time in the future you begin to feel less confident or a little down in the dumps, use the same after-shower lotion and repeat the procedure above. Any of the other products that were charged in the spell with pink light can also be used to instantly make you feel better about yourself.

To keep items charged, repeat the spell once a month, preferably under the new moon for growth.

SPELLS FOR HEALING

The following spells are used on a spiritual and energetic level to heal physical ailments in the body. These spells use herbs with both magickal and medicinal properties.

Chicken Soup Spell

Materials

- 2 cups (300 g) chicken soup (homemade is best, but canned works fine)
- Small pot
- Small sauté pan
- ½ clove garlic, minced
- 1 tablespoon butter or olive oil

Ritual

Pour the soup into the pot and heat to a low boil.

Lightly sauté the minced garlic in the butter or olive oil in a small pan. Add the minced garlic to the soup.

While it's cooking, stir the soup and chant:

"Cold, flu, and ills be gone.
Healthy body from now on."

Healing Poppet Spell

Materials

- 2 pieces of paper

  Scissors

- 1 pen

- 1 blue candle

- 2 tablespoons finely chopped peppermint leaves, either fresh or as dried tea (in a tea bag or loose)

- 2 tablespoons finely chopped fresh or dried rosemary

- 2 tablespoons finely chopped fresh or dried nettle leaf

  Fire-safe dish for burning the poppet

Ritual

Take the papers and roughly cut out two identical human shapes. On one, write the name of the person you wish to heal. On the other, write what it is they need healed. Layer the two pieces of paper, one on top of the other, with the writing on the outside. Light the candle and use the melted wax to start sealing the edges of the two pieces of paper together, creating a poppet (doll). Seal the poppet all the way around except for the head. Leave the head open and enough room in the body for the herbs.

Sprinkle the herbs inside the poppet, filling it until you feel satisfied. State:

"Poppet, I name you
(insert name of person who needs healing)."

Seal the poppet's head, and hold the poppet over the candle. Visualize the person's illness or ailment leaving their body. Concentrate, and feel a blue light filling that person. When you can no longer hold on to the visualization, place the poppet in the fire-safe dish and light the poppet on fire. As the poppet burns, chant:

"Fire burns the ill away,
Health and wellness here today."

When the fire is out, take the ashes outside and blow them into the four winds. Bury the candle leftovers at a crossroads or under a pine tree in your yard.

SPELLS FOR CLEANSING

In many spiritual healing practices, learning to cleanse your body and your house are essential ritual skills, as they help remove the buildup of negative energy that occurs through daily life. Everything we do generates energy. Cleansing the energy of our bodies and our houses releases built-up and toxic energy, allowing only beneficial energy to remain.

Kala Ceremony

The first cleansing ritual we will go through is called the Kala Ceremony—a ritual of cleansing with light. It comes from the Feri tradition of witchcraft as taught by American shaman Victor Anderson and his wife Cora Anderson.

Materials

Water

Drinking glass

Ritual

Pour some water into a glass and hold the glass in front of you. Start to focus deeply on all of the things that are stressful and upsetting in your life, and let yourself feel all the emotions within you that are attached to these issues. When your focus and emotions are at their most intense, place those emotions into your gut. Force the emotions out and into the glass in one large breath of air, almost like you are vomiting away all of the negativity within you and projecting it directly into the glass.

Imagine the negativity inside the glass transforming into a gray egg. As it sits in the water, envision the egg dissolving into a rainbow. Watch the water transform the negativity into a positive light. Once you see the rainbow of light, drink the water.

Feel the rainbow of light filling your entire body. See it removing any obstacles from your path. When you have consumed the water, say this spell:

"By the power of the rainbow light,
all negativity, frustrations, and anxieties are
transformed into energy that I can use for myself."

House-Cleansing Incense Spell

This spell is for an energetic washing of your home. The herbal wash mixture helps remove negative energy and replace it with positive energy and blessings.

Materials

- ¼ cup (70 g) sea salt (used to absorb heat)

  Censer or a fire-safe dish

- 1 charcoal disc (the small discs used to burn incense work well)

- 2 tablespoons finely ground angelica root

- 2 tablespoons finely ground lemon balm

- 2 tablespoons finely ground elderberry flowers

  Small bowl

- 1 feather

Ritual

Sprinkle a layer of salt onto the bottom of the censer or fire-safe dish. Place the charcoal disc on the salt, and light the charcoal. While the charcoal is sparking, mix the herbs together in the bowl to create a cleansing incense.

When the edge of the entire charcoal disc is glowing light red, slowly sprinkle the cleansing incense mixture on top of it. Carefully pick up the censer or fire-safe dish and walk to the front door. As you walk, use the feather to lightly waft the smoke toward the door. "Draw" a pentacle (a five-pointed star, also known as a pentagram) over the front door with the smoke, using the feather. As you draw the pentacle, state:

"Be gone negativity, Here now blessed be."

Walk along the edges of the room. Along every window and doorway, draw a pentacle and recite the chant. When you have completed the first room where the front door is, repeat the same process of drawing pentacles and walking the edges in every room in the house. When you have completed the process in all of the rooms, go to the living room. Stand in the center, and draw one more pentacle with the incense smoke. This time, see the pentacle grow large enough to surround the entire house. Place the censer and feather on the floor. Tap the floor with your foot three times and state:

"By my will, so shall it be.
Sealed now shall this cleansing be."

When the incense stops burning, the spell is complete. Scatter the remaining incense and charcoal onto the earth.

SPELLS FOR MONEY

One of the most common sources of stress in modern life is money. We need money to pay the bills, obtain food, and have shelter. We have all had financial worries at some point or another. Some people struggle with earning enough money or are out of work. Other people may have unexpected expenses come up in their lives, like medical or repair bills. All of these issues cause stress, and too much stress can lead to illness.

The following spells will help bring about a healthier bank balance and more peace of mind. Do be warned, though—casting spells for money will only bring about what a person actually needs, rather than what they desire: *Never spellcast for greed, only for what you need.*

Money-Packet Wish Spell

Materials

1 pen

1 green candle

1 sheet of paper

5 coins (4 pennies and 1 quarter, or
for other currencies

5 silver coins will work fine)

40 inches (100 cm) thin green ribbon
(giftwrapping style is fine)

Ritual

Using the pen, inscribe the wax of the candle with the word "money," and then, using the same pen, write the word "money" on the paper. Go on to write all of the things you need the money for, using as much detail as possible. For example, if you need extra funds to pay the bills, write clearly in capital letters:

GAS BILL, ELECTRIC BILL, MORTGAGE PAYMENT, DENTAL BILL, And so on.

As you write out your needs, pour your emotions into the paper. Place the coins on top of the paper, and light the green candle next to it. Say this spell seven times:

*"Like the trees growing free,
Prosperity there shall be."*

Keeping the coinage inside, start to fold the paper toward you, turning and folding the paper around the coins until you can't fold it anymore. Take the green ribbon and wrap it around the packet. With every three rotations of the ribbon-wrapping, turn the packet toward you and chant these words seven times:

"Money flowing free,
Prosperity there shall be.
Money worries gone from me."

When the packet is almost completely covered with the ribbon, use what's leftover to secure it with a knot. Drip wax from the candle onto the knot to seal the spell. Let the candle burn down, and bury any remains from it at the root of a tree near your home. Place the packet in your wallet or purse, or carry it in your pocket with you every day. If you wear a skirt or a dress, take a safety pin and pin the packet to the inside of your skirt or dress. Keep the packet with you until the money issues at hand have resolved. Then dispose of the packet at a crossroads or under a tree near your home.

Money-Tea Spell

Materials

Saucepan filled with water

Sharp knife

1 green candle

Copy of a utility bill or job application; anything that represents the need

Mortar and pestle

¼ teaspoon finely chopped chamomile flowers, either fresh or as dried tea (in a tea bag or loose)

2 teaspoons ground cinnamon

¼ teaspoon finely chopped goldenrod, either fresh or as dried tea (in a tea bag or loose)

Strainer

Mug or cup

1 tablespoon sugar

2 teaspoons honey

Candleholder

Ritual

Put the pan of water on the stove and bring it to a boil. While the water is heating up, use the knife to inscribe the candle with words of your intent ("erase debt," "find employment," "pay bills," etc.). Place the candle on top of a bill, job application, or a piece of paper with with your need written on it.

With the mortar and pestle, grind together the herbs and 1 teaspoon of the cinnamon for the tea. As you mix them, visualize your financial stress disappearing and your desire materializing. As the water on the stove boils, charge it with images of financial security and what manifestations of prosperity and success would look like. Visualize a green and orange light flowing in the water.

Put the blended herbs into the boiling water. Leave it to simmer for a few minutes. Take the pan off of the heat, and leave to cool. When the tea is cool enough, dip your finger into it and anoint the unlit candle. The candle should stay sitting on top of the bill, application, or paper. Say this spell five times:

"Money flowing free,
Money come to me."

Pick up the candle and rub it a few times from bottom to top with your hand. Strain the tea into a cup and then mix in a teaspoon each of cinnamon, sugar, and honey. Repeat the chant five more times while you stir the tea clockwise. When you've finished, rub the candle down with the remaining honey, from the bottom to the top. Once the candle has been fully anointed with the honey, roll it in the remaining cinnamon and sugar. Next, place the candle in a holder and light it. Take a sip of the tea, then say this spell:

"Money tea, I drink thee.
Prosperity there shall be."

Drink the tea. When the candle burns down, take the wax and the strained herbs from the tea and bury them at a crossroads. If there are no crossroads available, a spot on your property or a plot of land is acceptable. You can toss them into the trash, but do so with a prayer or statement, so that it brings your intent to all corners of the world.

SPELLS FOR LOVE

It is in a human being's nature to crave love, which is one of the most powerful forces on the planet. The energy we emit when we project love can accomplish many things, as well as relieve depression, anger, anxiety, and more. When we know those around us love us, it gives us a great strength and a sense of comfort, which can help us feel confident and at peace with the world.

Love comes from deep within our core, and in many cases, we have no control over whom we love or to what depth we devote ourselves to certain individuals. This lack of control can often lead us into relationships that are not necessarily right for our well-being but that help us grow and develop spiritually. Witches believe that the universe preordains every single person whom you touch hands with in life. We learn something from every person we meet along our journey. Even the toughest of love affairs will teach us something, however small, and give us knowledge that we can exercise to improve our situations later in life.

Spellcasting for love comes with its own rules and regulations, and one key thing to remember is to never meddle with another person's free will. Having this rule firmly planted in our minds makes it easy for us to know whether we are stepping over the line or not. It's perfectly okay to spellcast for the well-being of someone we love or to attract new romance into our lives, but never manipulate a person to feel something against his or her will. This is not only unethical, but the power is so great that if we do wield our magick for our own personal gain, it can go on to have disastrous consequences.

A Sweet "Notice Me" Spell

This love spell stays within the walls of ethical safety and is about getting someone to notice you. You are not interfering with another's free will, just implanting an idea and a picture of yourself in the mind so he or she can act on it, should that person want to.

For this, you will need to have a specific person in mind, so before you begin the spell, concentrate on the person you desire for a few minutes. If you have a photograph of them, even better!

Materials

Sharp knife (a paper clip or pen tip can also be used)

1 red candle

Small plate

1–2 tablespoons cloves (ground is fine)

1–2 tablespoons nutmeg (ground is fine)

1–2 tablespoons sugar

Small bowl

Ritual

For about five minutes, sit quietly in a comfortable chair and visualize yourself and the other person together. Imagine you are sitting opposite each other, passing the time of day. Using the knife (or paper clip or pen tip), inscribe your name on the candle along with the words "bring love." Place the candle in the center of the plate and light it.

Mix the spices in the bowl, stirring with intent. Sprinkle the mixture in a circle around the base of the candle and say these words seven times:

*"In your mind you will see only me.
If love is to be, your will shall be free."*

As the candle burns down, see yourself full of red and pink light. Imagine yourself being loved by others. Let the candle melt down to its end. If the chosen person is to be your true love, he or she will contact you within a week from the day you cast the spell. If not, then sadly that person is not for you!

Small-Shell Love Charm

The following spell is to attract new love to you—one of great passion, fidelity, and tenderness. If done correctly, you will find a long and lasting relationship with someone who will love you for who you really are.

Materials

- 2 bivalve shells—such as clamshells—of the same size (you only need 1 of the 2 shells from each of the bivalves)
- Small bowl
- Water
- Small towel
- 1 teaspoon dried red rose petals

- 1 teaspoon dried lavender
- ½ teaspoon ground ginger
- 1¼ teaspoon ground ginseng
- 1 pink candle
- 20 inches (50 cm) red ribbon (giftwrapping style is fine) or thread

Ritual

Take a walk on a beach at low tide and search for two shells of roughly the same size. If you are not near a beach, you can buy shells or even use shells from clams that you buy at the supermarket.

Once you have your shells, they will need a light cleansing. Place them in a small bowl of water. As they soak, visualize them covered in a white, blessed light. As you pat them dry with the towel, visualize yourself surrounded with red light.

Mix all of the dried petals and herbs together, and then sprinkle them evenly into the shells.

Place the candle between the two shells, light it, and say this invocation twelve times:

"Fire's passions bring to me,
Someone to love me completely."

Very carefully, melt wax along the edge of the shells and press them together until the wax has dried. Tie the ribbon around the shells and secure with a bow.

Put the shells back beside the candle, and let the candle burn down. Carry this shell talisman with you at all times and you should find the love of your life. Once you have, open the charm and take the shells back to the sea where you found them. This will ensure that the love will be everlasting. If you bought the shells, once the spell has manifested, crush up the shells and sprinkle them around a tree near your house or at a crossroads. This ensures the love will have a strong foundation and last.

Reconnect-with-Someone Knot Charm

This spell is ideal for reconnecting to friends and family members with whom you have lost contact. It's for reigniting the flames of an old love, romantic or otherwise.

Materials

Photograph of the person you wish to reconnect with

Red pen

20 inches (50 cm) yellow ribbon

Ritual

On the back of the photograph, write the word "reconnect" in red pen, and then say this incantation:

"By paths shared,
Two hearts once divided,
Now become united."

Now take the ribbon and wrap it around the photograph. With every wrap around the photograph, tie a knot (the knot should be on the front side of the photograph, on top of the person in the picture you want to reconnect with). After each knot you tie and chant a line from the spell on the following page, in order, for a total of nine knots.

"By round of one the spell's begun, {tie knot}
By round of two our relationship to renew, {tie knot}
By round of three so must it be, {tie knot}
By round of four apart no more, {tie knot}
By round of five this spell's alive, {tie knot}
By round of six this spell I fix, {tie knot}
By round of seven the spell reaches heaven, {tie knot}
By round of eight I create this fate, {tie knot}
By round of nine our love is fine." {tie knot}

Carry the charm with you until you are reconnected with the person you miss.

SPELLS FOR PROTECTION

There are times when it is vital that we protect ourselves magickally. The spells below will work for basically any kind of protection, be it safe travel, protection for the home, protection against psychic attack, or general all-around protection when you are away from home.

Black-Salt Protection for the Home

Materials

2–3 charcoal discs (the small discs used to burn incense work well)

Mortar and pestle

2 cups (550 g) sea salt

½ cup (approximately 20 leaves) white sage

¼ cup (or one large root) galangal root, chopped

¼ cup (25 g) bearberries (*Arctostaphylos uva-ursi*)

2 tablespoons black peppercorns

Ritual

Place the charcoal in the mortar and grind it with the pestle. If it is too hard, add a little water. This will soften the charcoal, making it easier to grind.

Add the other ingredients and thoroughly grind everything into a powder that resembles black salt. Sprinkle the mixture first on all your windowsills and then around the base of your doorways while visualizing a large shield over your home. Also scatter it into each corner of every room in your home. Feel the house being protected by an energetic field. As you go, say this spell in each room:

"Protection comes this way,
All negativity banished this day."

Repeat once a month, sweeping up the previous batch of salt before resetting a new batch.

Onyx Protection Pocket Charm

Materials

- ¼ teaspoon dragon's blood powder (a type of ground red resin made from several different plants; it is available at metaphysical shops or online)
- 1 small onyx stone

Ritual

Sprinkle the dragon's blood powder over the onyx stone. Visualize the energy from the dragon's blood charging the stone. Hold the stone in your hands and feel a shield surrounding yourself. Say this spell three times:

"Stone of shining black,
Protect me from any attack."

For all-around protection, carry the stone with you in your pocket.

PSYCHIC DEVELOPMENT SPELLS

The power of the mind is important in magick and witchcraft. The following spells are designed to help develop your psychic strength. By doing this, you can be in tune with your complete self in mind, body, and spirit.

Pocket Stone Charm

Materials

1 small amethyst crystal

8-9 drops lavender essential oil

Ritual

Drip the lavender oil in the shape of a pentacle over the amethyst. As you draw the pentacle, say this spell:

"Psychic abilities flowing free,
Psychic sight, come to me."

Add a few drops of oil to your finger and draw a pentacle on your forehead. (Please make sure you have no allergies to the oil before beginning this process.) Repeat the chant. The crystal will now be charged. At night, place the crystal under your pillow to help develop your psychic abilities and open your mind to lucid dreaming.

Mind-Clearing Crystal Water

Materials

1 of each of the following stones:
   Sodalite
   Lapis lazuli
   Clear quartz

   Clear drinking glass

   Spring water, enough to fill the glass

   Spray bottle

Ritual

Hold your hand over each stone, feeling your energy and the energy of the stones uniting. Place the stones in the bottom of the clear glass and add the spring water. Hold your hands over the crystal water and recite this chant five times:

"Cloudy thoughts flee quickly.
Crystals strengthen clarity.
Strength of mind, come to me."

Place the glass in direct sun for three hours, either outside or on a sunny windowsill, then remove the crystals from the glass. Pour the charged water into the spray bottle.

Spray the water onto your third eye (center of the forehead) and temple points. This will magickally give you mental clarity. Store the bottle in a cool and dark place so you can use it again in the future.

Prayers and Inspirational Sayings

As we stated earlier in this chapter, spellcraft is just one of the magickal tools in a witch's tool kit. Those who practice magickal spirituality are just like anyone else who follows a faith—they use ritual and prayer as tools to deal with life issues. We would like to thank our online friends for allowing us to share here their inspiring words, prayers, and spells that have empowered and inspired people across the globe.

Prayers are wishes and petitions for changes or needs that are spoken without any other direct ritual actions. Spells are petitions or prayers with actions taken to obtain your desire (such as writing your name on a candle, tying knots, and so on). You can end either a prayer or a spell with "So mote it be" if you wish.

Angel Greer

By the love of Hecate, Lady of Darkness and protector of her children, may you find relief of your ailments in her blessings.

As I will so, so mote it be.

Yvonne Beaver

We all have a gift in life; my gifts are a love of life and staying positive. Find your gift and stay positive! It may be as simple as making cookies or [sharing] a beautiful smile. It doesn't have to be a big thing, just something you do well and do with love.

Ginger Burkey

My favorite spell that I have done lately is a very simple positivity spell. It was for my job at a restaurant; our kitchen was not united and [the atmosphere was] very negative!

I got a glass jar and filled it with dried flower petals from a bouquet given to our kitchen (love), added lavender (peace), cinnamon (passion), and put a little something from each of us into the jar. Then I said:

"Goddess, please take the negativity out of our kitchen. Replace it with positivity, love, and teamwork! So mote it be!"

I repeated it three times. It has worked amazingly! When we get a new employee, I add something of theirs into the positivity jar and repeat my spell.

Liz Carney

We are of many different pagan paths that share the love and light we have together. Without judgment, we are a family on our own journey of discovery.

Kenya Coviak

This spell is called the Defensive Rogation of the Witch. It is a spell for settling the scales of justice or for defending against a curse.

"Into black wings, I encase my soul,
To ferry me to the halls of the just.
Barbs and lances, I entreat,
And dread eyes burn the dust and peat.
An arm, a blade, a thrash of blood,
A fire of pain and warding,
Rain down upon my ebon shields.
The ruby glints of forging,
I make upon the cold stone place,
My weapon, my tower, my stair,
And on my battlements screaming rage,
And hosts of things that bite and tear,
You will not breach these deathly walls.
Your curse breaks and burns bright,
I invoke the law of defense of I,
And return tenfold your blight."

Leanna Greenaway

You must always gaze up at the moon, for a true witch knows exactly when it's the right time to cast a spell!

Bronwyn Le Fae

I have always been a person of the people, all people. I'm inspired every day, and if we truly look, many of us are very alive inside. I see empathy in all walks of life.

I'm many voices for the people and of our wildlife, who do not have a voice. Our planet screams for our guardians to rise up to heal and cleanse the waters and earth. I have hope for the human race. I still believe my heart beats with the rhythm of life.

Karen Kasinskas

I have taken my knowledge in a new direction . . . Facebook! My goal is to reach as many people as possible and spread the joy and love of being Wiccan and pagan. I am truly blessed for all the people in my life! So many are like-minded, and as a crone I am still learning. . . . The best advice I give people having a hard time is [that] it's just a feeling, and it will pass. Tomorrow is a new day, a new beginning,

"I embrace our Mother Earth wholeheartedly,
And love walks in the woods, and meditation
    for grounding is a must.
Just know you were born with potential,
You were born with goodness and trust,
You were born with ideals and dreams,
You were born with greatness,
You were born with wings.
You were not meant for crawling, so don't.
You have wings; learn to use them and fly.
Don't ask yourself what the world needs,
Ask yourself what makes you come alive,
And then go and do that,
Because what the world needs is people
    who have come alive.
Blessed be."

Jamie Mendez

There is an ancient magick within you that is just waiting to erupt. Strip away the limiting beliefs that have been impressed upon you by this world, and watch your magick shine as your wild, unbridled self awakens.

Ceane O'Hanlon-Lincoln

Years ago, I wrote my own life's credo: "Thoughts are magick wands, powerful enough to make anything happen—anything we choose!" Wield that wand like a faerie godmother. You have the power! You have always had the power! Think about what you want, and it will manifest, because the real magick is believing in yourself!

Cary Pizarro

Spirit helps me through my tribulations, helps me walk my path with honor, helps me live in truth, gives me strength to see myself through my pain. Spirit's love reminds me I'm not alone; in my sadness I feel the goddess's embrace and Gaia offer me her bounties for protection and substance. The universe greeted me with the phases of the moon to work my magick.

Angela Scheppler Whiteman

This is an all-inclusive healing prayer:

> "Sisters, awake, long past time to end this break.
> One by one, reach out to those you trust,
> Sisters in common, arise from the dust,
> Reach out together to form as one.
> There is much work that needs to be done,
> Blessed goddess, hear my plea,
> In love and honor, so mote it be."

Sherry Tapke

This is a daily affirmation and prayer to your higher self to be the best you can be:

"I am in service to the light.
My brain controls my body, and I control my brain.
My body is healthy, youthful, and free of disease.
As I say, so it will be."

Sheila Sager

For a protection spell for police on duty,
trace a pentacle on the hood of their patrol car while saying:

"As I draw this pentacle here,
I call upon earth, fire, water, and air,
Protect this vehicle and all within,
From shift beginning to duty shift end."

Robert Vilches

In life, there will always be tragedies, chaos, and challenges. What we must do is balance negativity and find the good things in all situations. Change the world by living in love, unconditionally. Embrace evolution.

Dru Ann Welch

A prayer for personal daily healing and cleansing:

> "I am a vessel of healing. I am centered in my heart space.
> With each breath in, I am filled with golden healing light,
> Light as bright as the sun.
>
> It fills my entire being, bringing healing to each cell.
> With each breath out, I release all darkness
> and negativity, all that no longer serves me.
> So mote it be."

Lashette Williams

I say this over and over as I gently and patiently pull the comb through my curls:

> "Remove obstacles, discard negativity,
> Untangle my thoughts so that I can have a good day."

Heidi Wolfson

I believe strongly that we create our own reality and what you put into the universe is what you get back. Therefore, the thought, the act, the deed, and the intention are what make magick come to life. We are the vessels keeping the power alive. Magick passes through us like the air we breathe. It is conscious, and, as a result, our motivation is what creates our reality.

Tracie (Sage) Wood

This is a simple cleansing and protection prayer for your house:

"Attacks be gone, attacks away,
On this land you have no sway.
For those of you that seek to harm,
I call the goddess to disarm.
By the power of Kali and mighty Hecate,
Towers of steel, shield of strength be,
Keep me and mine safe within.
No harm, no foul, no evil shall win,
Tides will turn against the foe.
The wind shall carry this, I know,
Keep all safe, from thee to me,
As I will, so mote it be."

Shawn Robbins

You are destiny's child, a shining star in the universe illuminating the path for others.

Charity Bedell

You can make your dream come true. You have the strength and power within you. Use the power of your dreams to work magick and manifest your reality. The power is yours.

Believe.
So mote it be.

Chapter 5

Healing Candles, a Sacred Flame

CANDLE MAGICK, RITUALS, AND SPELLS

Wiccans know that candles are some of the most powerful objects in a witch's toolbox. Lighting a candle and reciting a chant or prayer for enlightenment, empowerment, and good health is one use. The candle also has the power to ward off negative energy and impart positive energy into one's life. By learning how to harness the candle's mysterious and magickal power—and believing in the magick within ourselves to change our world for the better—we can lead richer, fuller, and more fulfilling lives.

CANDLE MAGICK

The very first spell that almost everyone casts is the one we perform on our birthdays. Someone lovingly bakes or buys a cake, and candles representing our age are placed on the top. These candles are lit, and as we close our eyes and blow them out, we are told to make a silent wish. Many believe that this tradition dates back to ancient pagan rituals. Our birthdays were considered all-important, as they mark our entry into this world. This made for a magickal day. The candles on the cake held a great force and power, and once blown out, the wish was then carried by the smoke and sent directly to the gods. The gods, in turn, would receive the message and grant the wish.

Candles are integral to spellcasting. If you are new to magick, candle spells are probably the best way to get started. Most of us have a supply of candles in a cupboard, and many people will often light one at night while having dinner or chilling out in front of the TV. But what many people don't realize is that a candle symbolizes the elements of earth, air, water, and fire (the earth is represented by the wax before it is burned, air by the smoke from the burning candle, water by the melted wax, and fire by the flaming wick), and if you want to cast a wish out to the universe, all you need is the fire and the spirit to make it happen.

Whether you choose to cast magick the traditional way or with a more modern approach, most spells work best with a candle at hand. The most important thing is to first understand how the magick of the candle works and what things are likely to influence the spell and make it successful.

With any kind of magick, you must first make sure that you are in the right frame of mind. If you are in a bad mood, feeling unhappy, or are ailing, then casting any kind of spell will result in the opposite of the intended effect.

For most candle rituals, it is best to allow the candle to burn down on its own. Only when the candle has extinguished itself will the spell be complete. There are spells in circulation that have you extinguish the flame after a specific burning time and then relight it the following day, but with most rituals, if it is blown out early, the spell is lost.

For safety reasons, of course, you should never leave a candle unattended while you head off to bed or to another room, so choosing the right size and shape of candle, as well as one with a reasonable burning time, is important. Tall, tapered candles can take up to nine hours to burn, whereas large chubby candles can take days. Many times, it makes better sense to use a tea light or a small, thin candle with a burning time of around three to four hours. These give the spells a decent amount of time to simmer without encroaching too much on your own time. All of these smaller varieties can easily be found in local stores or purchased on the Internet.

Candle Colors and Their Magickal Correspondences

One of the most important parts of candle magick is using the right color candle, as the correct color will often make all the difference to the outcome. Some spells are rigid and need a precise color or shade of a color, while others are more open-ended. If you are in doubt about what color to use, always use a white candle. This is a neutral and pure color that can be used when you are not sure of what color would be best for a spell or if you are out of the color candle specified in your spell. Following is a list of the main candle colors and their correspondences:

WHITE

Cleansing homes

Purifying spaces

Creating harmony

Invoking spirits

Improving communication with others

Summoning guides and angels

For use in every situation

BLUE

Promoting restful sleep

Finding the truth

Gaining wisdom and knowledge

Invoking psychic visions

Calming emotions

Suppressing anger

Aiding meditation

Moving your house

Becoming more patient with others

Curing a fever

Having a better understanding

Protection

RED

Promoting strength and vigor

Rejuvenating energy and stamina

Conjuring willpower

Summoning courage

Inciting passion and sexual love

Sparking enthusiasm

Prompting quick results

Warding off enemies

Becoming more attractive to others

PINK

Healing emotions

Attracting romance

Becoming more caring

Inviting peace and tranquility

Healing rifts

Banishing selfish emotions

Protecting family and friendships

Invoking spiritual healing

Being more compassionate

GREEN

Accumulating money and wealth

Promoting prosperity and abundance

Accomplishing goals

Growing plants

Attracting luck

Negotiating employment matters and finding new jobs

Hastening conception and solving fertility issues

Casting out greed and resentment

YELLOW

Increasing activity

Resolving health matters

Nurturing creativity and imagination

Passing exams and learning

Aiding concentration

Controlling mood swings

Protecting yourself
when traveling

Persuading others

Healing problems
associated with
the head

ORANGE

Increasing energy and
stamina

Improving the mind and
memory

Promoting success and
luck

Developing business and
career

Helping those with new
jobs

Clarifying legal matters
and justice

Selling goods or houses

Capturing a thief or
recovering lost
property

Removing fear

PURPLE

Summoning spirit help

Bringing peace,
tranquility, and
harmony

Improving psychic ability

Aiding astral projection

Healing

Easing sadness

Improving male energy

Summoning spiritual
protection

BROWN

Attuning with the trees
and earth

Promoting concentration

Helping with decisiveness

Protecting animals

Amplifying assertiveness

Aiding friendships

Bringing material gain

Gaining mental stability

Connecting with Mother
Nature

Studying and learning

SILVER

Summoning the Mother
Goddess

Drawing down the moon

Connecting with lunar
animals

Purifying female energy

Improving all psychic
abilities

Aiding clairvoyance and

the unconscious mind

Ridding negativity

Developing intuition

Interpreting messages in
dreams

Banishing bad habits

GOLD

Healing and enhancing
well-being

Rejuvenating yourself

Improving intelligence

Bringing financial gain
and wealth

Winning competitions

Attracting love and
happiness

Maintaining peace in
families

Cosmic ordering

BLACK

Protection

Strength

Banishing

Reversal

Hex-breaking

Choosing and Cleansing Your Candles

It is important that you magickally disinfect your candles before use. Many candles are mass-produced across the world, often in less-than-ideal conditions, and because wax is a vessel for energy, every single person that came into contact with your candle—be it the candlemaker or the person who packed it in a box—will have deposited some of their energy onto the wax. If you have the inclination, it would be best to make your own candles from scratch, but few of us have the time or the equipment to do this.

Store-bought candles are perfectly acceptable, but try and avoid ones that are dipped, meaning that the maker dipped a white candle into colored wax. This is fine if you just want to burn pretty colors in your home, but for magickal purposes, it's far better to use ones that are a solid color throughout.

There are many different ways to cleanse your candles before a spell, but you have to find a method that suits you. Some people enjoy a prolonged ceremony of candle cleansing and will even leave their candle outside for a week in the garden to soak up the moon's rays. Others just want to do a minimum amount of preparation. Here is an example of candle cleansing that sits somewhere in the middle and works perfectly well.

The term we use for this cleansing is called *anointing*, and it involves water and oils to prepare the candle before the ritual begins.

Step 1: Wipe Clean
Wipe the wax with a paper towel, removing all traces of debris and dust.

Step 2: Prepare a Solution
Purchase a small bottle of spring water and pour into a saucepan. Add one teaspoon of sea salt, and warm until the salt dissolves. Allow the

water to cool before pouring it back into the bottle. You can keep this water in the fridge for about a month for use in future preparations.

Step 3: Intent

Standing in front of the sink, hold the candle in your left hand, which is nearer to your heart. Being careful not to wet the wick, pour a small amount of the saline-water solution over the candle. If you are using a tea-light candle to cut down on burning time, remove the candle from its casing before cleansing with the water. Take a fresh paper towel and dry thoroughly while saying the following invocation:

"This magickal water cleanses thee,
With good intent and purity."

Step 4: Inscribing

With a small, sharp paring knife or a thick needle, scratch your full name and your wish into the wax—for example: "Jane Brown, to lose weight." It doesn't matter where you inscribe your words on the candle, and it is not very important that it is even legible. Once the candle is lit, these words will burn away, giving the spell more clout.

Step 5: Anointing

Pour some pure vegetable oil (the kind you would cook with) into a small bowl or eggcup. Vegetable oil is used as a base oil for most anointing, but for spells relating to health and well-being, you can mix in a few drops of other oils if you wish. Lavender is often used with healing and well-being spells and will intensify the magick even more. Hold the candle in your left hand again. Dip the first finger of your right hand into the oil and run it down the candle from top to bottom in a line. To anoint a tea light, place it back in its casing, dip your finger into the oil, and smear it in a clockwork motion around the top of the candle wax. Say this invocation:

"This magickal oil anoints thee, With all things good, magickally."

The candle is now cleansed, charged, and ready to be placed in a suitable holder in preparation for your spell.

Step 6: Rhyming and Repetition

One of the ways we can add more punch to a spell is by repeating the incantation over and over. Often, prewritten spells, both ancient and modern, will rhyme with some kind of poetic fluidity. As we mentioned previously, saying a spell repeatedly helps to enforce the message, which, in turn, gives it more power each time it is spoken. Generally, a spell is recited no less than three times in a row. You may notice that some have greater repetitions, such as seven, nine, or even twelve times. These are considered to be the most magickal numbers and represent completion.

Step 7: Ending the Spell

After repeating your spell the desired number of times, you will need to close the ritual. Choose one of the phrases below to say before looking upward and saying thank you.

"And so it is."
"The spell is cast."
"So mote it be."

PREPARATION
FOCUSING ON THE MAGICK WITHIN

Before you cast a candle spell, sit quietly in a comfortable chair for about fifteen minutes. Hold your unlit candle in both hands and think about your wish long and hard. Begin to visualize its positive outcome. For example, if your demeanor is sluggish and your desire is to be more energetic, close your eyes and imagine yourself running very quickly across a great expanse. Concentrate on this deeply. Feel the wind on your face and the vigor in your body. After five minutes of this, switch your visualization to a large trampoline. Climb onto it and begin jumping, gently at first, before going higher and higher. You are free of any aches and pains, your ailments have left you, and your vitality is immense. In your mind's eye, see an image of yourself being the very best you can be.

Sometimes even just a brief meditation like this can leave you feeling refreshed and invigorated.

CANDLE SPELLS FOR HEALING AND WELL-BEING

Here we share ten spells for physical and mental health and happiness. (Note, however, that you can magickally alleviate almost any problem by adapting the general health spell on page 142 to suit your need.) The basis for each ritual is the same, and a yellow candle will suffice for any ailment or disability, as this is the assumed color used for healing. White, orange, silver, and gold are also appropriate colors and will not adversely affect the results. When you have chosen the color, prepare the candle as described in the previous section by inscribing it with the sufferer's name and the nature of the illness. For example, if you have an ingrown toenail that you want to heal, inscribe the words "Sarah Brown" and "heal ingrown toenail" onto the wax before anointing and lighting it.

You will notice that there are lots of different anointing oils listed in the spells below, but basil oil is often used for healing. If you cannot find this or have a problem getting out and about, you can use plain vegetable oil as a substitute. The addition of certain herbs and oils are optional. A simple candle ritual without the oils will suffice and be just as effective with the right intent, but these extras can enhance the magick and allow the outcome to come about much more quickly.

Call on the Angels

Many spellcasters like to invoke the power of angels. There are trillions of angels in the spirit world, each one with the power to help any problematic situation that may arise. One of the most powerful is the archangel Raphael. He is the predominant healer in the angelic realm, and many people find that when they call upon his power, their spells are more successful and their prayers are answered. To invoke his power, you could place a white feather on your workspace and say this incantation before you begin casting your spell:

> "Archangel Raphael, healer of mankind,
> I ask your assistance this day.
> Encircle me with your powerful light,
> Love and protect me, come what may.
> Envelop me with the warmth of your wings,
> As I cast this spell while the angel sings."

A General Spell for Better Health

This spell can be used and adapted for any health problem you might have or to simply keep you in great shape all year round. Prepare a yellow candle. Inscribe it with your name and the words "good health." Blend one tablespoon of vegetable oil and nine drops of basil oil to promote vigor. Anoint the candle with this oil and place in a safe holder. Sprinkle some protective salt in a circle around the base of the holder and light the candle. Say this spell three times:

> "Surround my being in positive rays,
> Encompass me and bless my being,
> Shower healing light so that I might
> Stay fit and well in the coming days."

Let the candle burn down, and repeat the spell once a month to insure overall good health.

To Remove Fear and Phobias

If you have an inner fear you want to conquer, prepare an orange candle and inscribe it with your name and the words "remove my fear." Anoint the candle with plain vegetable oil. Place a picture that represents your phobia next to it and light it. Rose quartz prevents worry, so hold a piece in your hand and say this spell seven times:

"With this crystal, remove my fear,
With this candle, settle here,
See this photo and make it be
An agreeable thing for me to see."

Place the crystal next to the candle and leave it until the candle burns out. Once it has, tear up the photo, put it in the trash bin, and place the crystal under your pillow for seven nights.

To Cure Insomnia

If you are the kind of person who watches the clock go around and around at night without drifting off, this spell will help bring about peaceful sleep. In the early evening, prepare a purple candle, and inscribe your full name and the words "to cure insomnia" into the wax. Anoint the candle with pure lavender oil. This will induce sleep. Place it on a table in your bedroom. Add a bowl of freshly dried lavender to the table, and sprinkle a few drops of lavender oil on the herbs. Say this spell three times:

"Sleepy slumber, peaceful rest,
I am protected, I am blessed.
Beside my head tonight I keep
These magickal herbs to aid my sleep."

Settle down into bed with a good book. Once the candle has burned down, you can go to sleep. Leave the lavender in place somewhere in your bedroom so the magick can continue to work over the coming months. This spell might need refreshing every few months if its effects begin to wear off.

Headaches, Migraines, and Sinus Problems

For those who suffer constantly with head-related problems, this spell will clear the mind and release any blockages or tension that cause pain or discomfort. Use a white candle, and inscribe it with your full name and the words "clear my head." Anoint the candle with pure eucalyptus oil and place in a holder. Make a cup of feverfew tea—a plant renowned in herbology for curing headaches—either from tea bags or with five to six leaves from the plant. Place the tea on the table and light the candle. Repeat the following invocation nine times:

> *"Clear my head, release my pain,*
> *So I can be healthy once again.*
> *With magickal power I bless this tea,*
> *Dispel this ache, remove from me."*

When the candle has burned for around twenty minutes, drink the tea, then allow the candle to burn all the way down. If you suffer from serious migraine attacks, you will have to cast this spell regularly.

Preventing Colds, Flus, and Viruses

If people around you are suffering from contagious illnesses and you want to protect yourself from their germs, cast this spell in the early evening. Prepare a blue candle, and inscribe it with your name and the words "protect me from illness." To anoint the candle, blend a teaspoon of vegetable oil with four drops of citronella oil to protect you from and block out ailments. Place in a suitable holder and set aside. Light one cedar incense stick. This will magickally charge you and give you strength. Next, light the candle and say this spell twelve times:

"Protect me from illness all around,
A magickal shield from my head to the ground.
This virus will not pass through me,
For I am strength, so mote it be."

Fertility Spell

This spell should help most childless couples, but it will work better if both of the potential parents perform the magick. Basil is renowned for possessing fertility properties, and when used in fertility spells, it tends to magickally charge itself, changing energies from barren to fruitful. On a full phase of the moon, purchase a large bunch of basil and tie the stalks together with a length of red ribbon. Place the basil on a worktop and bless three candles—one pink, one blue, and one green—and inscribe

each one with the word "fertility." Anoint the candles with pure basil oil. Situate the candles around the basil and light them. Repeat the following invocation twelve times:

"From fruitful seed, we shall breed,
From a sterile womb, a baby soon.
With the basil we give, a child shall live,
Hear my plea, bring life to me."

Leave the candles to burn down and then tie the basil over your bed. Make love under the basil for seven nights.

Banishing Bad Habits and Addictions

This is a general spell that uses two candles and is meant for any kind of bad habit, ranging from nail biting to smoking to overindulgence of food or drink, all the way to drug addiction. Whether this is a spell you want to perform for yourself or you are concerned about a loved one, in order for the magick to work, it's very important to get the candle inscriptions right. You must inscribe the full name of the person for whom you want to cast the spell on both candles. You must also inscribe a brief description of the habit you want to break on both candles.

For example, if you want to lose weight, you would inscribe "Jane Brown, to lose weight," or "Jane Brown, to quit smoking." You can easily adapt this spell to suit your situation, so feel free to play with the wording, as long as it is specific. You must also have an object present next to the candle that represents the bad habit. If the issue is a food addiction, your favorite kind of chocolate bar would suffice. If you are a smoker and want to quit, use a pack of cigarettes.

To prepare the oil for anointing, steep two whole, peeled garlic cloves in two tablespoons of vegetable oil overnight. The next day, prepare one white and one black candle with your inscription, and anoint them in the usual way. Place them on a work surface, and situate the object representing the habit next to them. Light the candles and say this spell twelve times:

"I banish the black with all that is right,
Protection will come with the flame on the white.
I banish this habit with love and with light,
With all that is good and all that is bright."

Leave the candles to burn down and then bury the offending object in the garden or in a pot full of soil. If you get the urge to reach for your habit, repeat the above spell over and over until the moment has passed.

Calming Anger or Bitterness

No matter if you are a petulant individual in general or if you suffer from bouts of anger, this spell will help you to chill out and calm down. You can also cast this spell on behalf of someone else; if you have a friend or family member that is out of control with moody or aggressive behaviors, you can help ease their agitated mindset. Prepare a yellow candle and inscribe it with the full name of the sufferer and the words "to calm anger." Mix one tablespoon of vegetable oil with ten drops of rose oil and three drops of sage oil. Anoint the candle in the usual way. You will also need a lock of the sufferer's hair. If you want to perform this spell without the person knowing, a few strands of their hair from a hairbrush or comb will be sufficient.

Light the candle and say this spell three times:

"When anger comes, I silence the rage,
With candles bathed in rose and sage.
From hatred to joy, I make the shift,
The manner is sweet, the mood will lift."

Take a few strands of the hair and singe them in the flame, then let the candle burn down.

Back Problems

Many people suffer from back problems, and this can often be the manifestation of a metaphor: that we are carrying too much on our shoulders. This spell will release tension in the back and settle down any trapped nerves or soreness. Cleanse a pink tea-light candle, and inscribe the sufferer's name into the wax with the words "heal back pain." Blend a tablespoon of vegetable oil and four drops of ginger oil for anointing. Scatter one cup of sea salt onto a dish, place the candle on top, and light it. Using the meditation technique described earlier in this chapter (see page 139), visualize yourself in perfect health, free of pain, and physically active. Say the following incantation seven times:

> *"I charge this salt with a powerful force,*
> *In the hope that I will be back on course.*
> *The healing grains shall ease my pain,*
> *And very soon I'll be well again."*

When the candle has burned down, draw a warm bath and scatter the salt into the water. The healing power of the salt bath twinned with the magick of the spell will have you feeling in tip-top condition in no time.

Dealing with Unhappy Emotions and Stress

Sometimes, and often for no good reason, we can all get a bit down in the dumps. There might be a specific situation causing the blues, or you may be suffering minor depression from hormonal flux or other physical reasons. Whatever the cause, this spell will help lift the black cloud that is overhead and help you feel more content. It will also combat any stress you might be feeling and help to calm anxiety. Cleanse a small brown candle and anoint it with pure peppermint oil. This oil is very useful for clearing the mind and helping us see things more plainly. Scratch your name into the wax along with the words "ease my sadness." Place the candle next to a piece of smoky quartz crystal and say this spell three times:

"Despondent thoughts, leave my mind,
My inner peace, soon I'll find.
Erase this mood and leave me free,
To be contented with life and truly happy."

Leave the smoky quartz in situ until the candle has finished burning and then carry the crystal with you for at least a few weeks. You should start to feel better almost immediately, but if for whatever reason you find it takes a little longer to lift your mood, repeat the spell each night and sleep with the smoky quartz next to your bed.

Aromatherapy Candles

BY STEVIE PAPOI

Candles do more than just keep the darkness at bay. While that is important, they can also be used for better health and a more rewarding life. I am talking about using specialized candles designed for aromatherapy and magickal spell work. Aromatherapy stimulates your memory, circulation, and endocrine glands, heling you live a healthier life. Aromatherapy candles are normally made from an all-natural wax, such as soy or beeswax. These candles are designed to use essential oils to trigger your olfactory receptor cells, which in turn send a signal to the part of your brain known as the limbic system. If you have any medical conditions, you should consult a medical professional before starting any aromatherapy program.

Another type of popular aromatherapy is a massage candle, made from soy wax carefully blended with a carrier agent and essential oil, which, when melted, can be massaged into your skin like lotion. These specialized candles have oils that can be absorbed through the skin. The oils then spread their healing energy throughout your entire body.

I believe what draws people to candle magick is that it's a

reasonably priced and uses materials that are readily available, and, well, everyone loves candles. Candle magick allows you to feel a real connection to your craft as you carve magickal words and symbols representing your desire into the wax and anoint the candle for use. Each step empowers the candle to help your spell manifest. Actually seeing the candle burning and smelling the aroma triggers your olfactory system. As you see the candle melt, you see your spell being projected. When I am asked about candles for healing spells, I recommend using a light-blue candle for mental-health issues and a dark-blue candle for physical health issues. White candles are used to cleanse the body and spirit.

CREATING YOUR OWN MAGIC

Often the best and most successful spells are those written by the caster herself. If you are a creative sort, you might like to have a go at writing some of your own. It all comes back to the intent and the focus on what you want. (Says Charity: Whenever I want a parking space, I simply say, "I desire a parking space" three times. It always works!) If you take the time and energy to devise the ritual from scratch, the odds are good that your spell will hold more clout.

With the abundance of information we have around us online today, it is quite easy to research the properties of herbs, flowers, and other natural resources that you can use in your own spells.

Hopefully, you will have learned from this book how to cleanse and prepare a candle. The other items present on your altar or workspace can be adapted to suit the spell at hand. When you come to write your incantation, just make sure that it is specific to what you want. It is good if a spell rhymes, because when you recite the wording over and over again, it will flow well. It's not imperative to have a diploma in poetry; just say what you want and repeat it several times. Give it a go, and good luck making that magick happen!

Chapter 6

Spiritual Alchemy and Holistic Enlightenment

SUMMON
YOUR INNER
LIGHT

We are all on a spiritual journey, looking within ourselves for insight and outward to the stars for answers to why we are here on Earth, where we are going, and what our purpose is in life. Some of us take a road less traveled to get there, while others follow a tried-and-true religious path. No matter which road you are on, the ultimate destination is still the same: finding your way home to that sacred place of spiritual being.

WHAT IS SPIRITUALITY?

There are many religions, faiths, deities, and different points of view, but one constant thread in most religious teachings is the power of spiritual enlightenment to reach the highest level of our being—Buddhists refer to this as Nirvana, though others may simply think of this as being the best humans we can be, pure in our intentions and emotions.

In the words of Rob Jones, cofounder (with John "Tip" Masssaro) of the Facebook group Practitioners of the Craft,

Think of it as a vast sea of energy that is in all aspects of our existence. A source of energy that animates all things; everything is a part of it. We as people feel a connection to it and have given it many names and labels, one of which is god. We seek to have a better understanding of it, we connect with it (if so inclined), and we work with it and honor it as sacred. So for as many different cultures as there have been and as many viewpoints differ, there are many different ways mankind has gone about understanding and relating to the source, so we've given it multiple names and identities that reflect the cultural background the concept originated in, and thus the deity was created.

All versions of gods out there are aspects of or masks for source energy. They use these concepts to communicate with people, to be understood. The purpose of spirituality is to find the divine within you and without you, so that you can affect change and achieve a more enlightened state of being.

There is no "right" or "wrong" way to pursue or find spirituality. When something fits with your beliefs, you will know it. You'll feel at peace, inspired to learn more, and ready to share what you know with others. This chapter takes a look at some of the spiritual paths that have been around for many, many moons. Maybe one—or more—will speak to you.

BUDDHISTS
LOVE AND LET LOVE

Buddhism is one of the most straightforward forms of spirituality and paths to spiritual growth. Like many other religions, Buddhists believe that we are all one, and as such, what one person does affects the other and vice versa. As part of one living, breathing life, we can never truly be free of one another, nor should we be. According to Buddhist thought, seeing a beggar lying in the street and ignoring him only harms yourself in the end, because it encourages others to also look away. But to reach out your hand to a beggar shows compassion and kindness and teaches others to do the same.

Therefore, the way to show love is to be kind to one another, throw away our judgments, and live in harmony with our fellow man. Note that this doesn't include pushing our own beliefs on the people around us or forcing them to be kind (as though any of us could do that—"Be nice or *else*!"). Rather, Buddhists lead by example. Kindness begets kindness. Compassion leads to more compassion. Living a spiritual life encourages others to follow suit.

Buddhists believe in the power of humanity and the power within the self to evolve, change, and share wisdom and knowledge with the rest of the world.

Ask any of the estimated 500 million people around the world who follow Buddhism what they believe, and the answers will be similar: they want to relieve suffering and unhappiness and replace it with supreme happiness and joy. Buddhists believe this process leads to the liberation of the soul and spiritual enlightenment. To be a Buddhist is an opportunity to fill your heart with gratitude and faith in humanity due to the simple fact that you will be able to inspire others to help those less fortunate than yourself and, in doing so, help lead those around you to a higher spiritual plane.

MYSTICISM, MYSTICS, AND THE KABBALAH

Kabbalah is a mystical interpretation of Judaism and the Hebrew Bible, a revealing source-wisdom in how we live, how we give, and how we receive. Kabbalah brings forth faith in the humanity, human kindness, and forgiveness that is in all of us. Followers set out on an inspirational journey—seeking to turn chaos into inner peace—a quest to find the true self and rid the self of emotional baggage. Because this idea is universal, it can resonate with anyone—young and old, rich and poor, male and female, and practitioners of all faiths. After all, we are all seekers of the light, trying to heal our inner souls and be free of the fire in our bellies that feeds on anger and prevents us from breathing in the fresh air of pure intention.

Kabbalah has its roots in teachings that are thousands of years old. At one time, only married, Jewish, male scholars had access to the texts associated with these teachings; now they are available for everyone to explore and learn from. Truth doesn't change, even over the course of several millennia, which is why Kabbalah's principles continue to inspire men and women around the world.

WITCHCRAFT AND SPIRITUAL WELL-BEING

For those who follow the path of the witch, history, magick, and lore are passed down from ancient ancestors, taught by elders, and practiced by those who follow the faith. When faced with life's problems, witches don't run away from them, nor do they hide and pretend their problems don't exist—they seek solutions and answers from their fellow sisters and brothers who have walked down that same long, winding road themselves.

Many Wiccans believe there is a direct relationship between the mind, the body, and the spirit. To be truly healed emotionally, physically, and spiritually, one has to treat all aspects of the mind, the body, and the spirit. If any one of them is out of alignment, they can all go out of sync. Everything is connected, and everything relates to being whole and one.

Herbs, natural remedies, and meditation are some of the holistic methods witches have used for hundreds of years to reach a heightened sense of awareness in an otherwise cluttered world. Once upon a time, those who practiced folk medicine and folk healing traditions were a central part of local communities, often revered as the healers of the village and sought out for advice on day-to-day ailments such as colds, flus, injuries, infections, and even problems like anxiety, depression, and insomnia.

It was the duty of these folk healers to find the root causes of maladies. It was a common belief that a spirit or spiritual issue could cause physical problems. Such troubles could be related to spirit injuries caused by possession, loss of spirit, and other supernatural events. For this reason, many of the methods used by true folk healers included not only medical treatments using herbal substances, but also spell work and formal ritual work. Their job was to address the person as a whole and identify the cause of the symptoms, as opposed to treating only the symptoms (which is what Western medicine primarily does today). These practices evolved into modern witchcraft practices, many of which are now becoming accepted into mainstream health care.

NATIVE AMERICAN SHAMANS
MEDICINE MEN AND WOMEN

One of the most well-known healing styles is practiced by the medicine men and women of the Native American traditions. These people are shamans who specialize in various healing techniques, from drumming work and deep-trance work to communicating on an otherworldly level.

Medicine in this practice is not "medicine" as we know it in mainstream culture today. The key to the shaman's magickal and spiritual healing is through his or her connection to the spiritual and energetic forces in the universe—the spiritual properties of plants, people, places, and objects. A medicine man or woman can feel the spiritual forces in the land and communicate with them for health and wellness. The emphasis in their healing practice is the unity between the spirit and the physical form.

One of the key components of shamanism is the ability to travel into the spirit world in a controlled setting. These out-of-body travels provide shamans with knowledge and wisdom and let them mediate the relationship between the physical and the spiritual. Using these techniques, shamans can face death, spirits of the underworld and the lands, their ancestors, and their gods.

One of the best-known tools for shamanic healing is the sweat lodge, a place for cleansing and purification rituals based on the idea that profuse sweating removes toxins from the body. The removal of the toxins also extends to the spiritual level, as it removes negative energy that may be causing issues and ailments. By removing forces that are damaging to your body and your spirit, more beneficial energies can come in and take their rightful place.

In some shamanic traditions, it is believed that when a person endures various traumas (and what defines a traumatic event is different for every person and every situation), a part of their spirit breaks off and becomes lost. Finding that soul fragment—in a ritual called *soul retrieval*—is one of the few ways to fully heal from those events. Soul retrieval is not an easy task, and it is often a very emotional process. Both the shaman and the trauma survivor need to work together to travel the landscape of the spirit world to find the missing part of the soul or spirit. It is only by regaining that soul fragment that a person can really be "whole" again.

Pagans:
It's All about Balance

BY DONNA MORGAN

Pagan teachings are all about equality and balance. We believe that all living things have a male and female aspect and that those aspects share equal responsibility. As the sun complements the moon, so this male/female rhythm exists in all things found in nature.

My Native American and druid Celt ancestors taught me the meaning of this balance with the gods. The gods and goddess have always ruled together, taking on shared responsibilities in their areas of knowledge to assist all beings to work in harmony with one another. This is the pattern, the recipe, for world and universal peace. Pagans believe that if it is not equal, it is not balanced.

We are meant to keep this balance in check. In fact, when this delicate setup is off-kilter, energies swing to extremes, causing chaos and disarray with all planets and lifeforms. When this happens, it is hard for us to find inner peace.

For many years, pagans have seen and felt this unbalance in the spiritual realm. "How do we fix this?" you may ask. It's an individual task, as each of us plays an intricate part in the whole system of restoring balance into this world—starting with our own personal space. Spirituality is not something you can buy or bargain for but something personal within yourself and your connections with the gods and goddesses.

This is an essential piece because there are other spiritual teachings that do not embrace the male/female aspects equally. So if you are wondering why your spiritual views are not meeting your needs, ask yourself if your male and female energies are in balance or if one is dominating your spiritual field. If you need more help, there are many pagan organizations and communities out there that offer this truth—seek them out. And if they try to dish up just one god or one goddess or are not embracing an equal part of both, they too have not found balance. Take your time and ask plenty of questions, for the truth will come if you truly seek it.

ROOTWORK, CONJURE, OR HOODOO

The African American practice of rootwork—also known as *conjure* or *hoodoo*—originated from West African religious customs and evolved into a naturalistic and spiritual tradition during the period of the American slave trade. Rootwork adherents believe that there is a spiritual force present in all things—plants, animals, minerals, and even places. This is a central component of the practice and the work that root doctors perform.

Another way they work is to use herbs, roots, and resins to make natural remedies. Africans knew all of their local plants and the various associations for healing that they held. This was not the case when they were brought as slaves to America, where all of the plants and resources were foreign and the vast majority of slaveholders were not concerned with the slaves' health or safety. In order to survive, they needed to find a way to make their own medicine and keep their spirits alive.

Native Americans were instrumental in the development of rootwork. Members of certain tribes, mostly in the South, shared their knowledge of healing herbs and their uses with enslaved African Americans.

As slavery came to an end and the African community was able to move north and intermingle with new cultures, other influences came into play. Elements of Jewish mysticism from the Kabbalah—such as the use of the psalms in the Bible and working with entities like Moses—entered into rootwork. Traditions from Appalachian folk magick, from the Pennsylvania Dutch (powwow and hex signs), and from other Germanic systems (practices involving runes and sigils) were added. In this way, rootwork developed several unique flavors across the country, all connected to the past in Africa and the new land in America.

Many people understand rootwork to simply be the working of magick and spiritual work with the use of plants. This is not the case. Rootwork is actually the ability to bring out the "root"—as in the spirit—of the plant and let it be an essential component of the work. There is no separation of the body and the spirit in this practice, as both are essential to well-being. In essence, root doctors believe that we are not our physical forms. We are spirits existing in a physical form.

The process of calling out the root of plants, stones, or crystals is called "doctoring," and it is one of the main ways that the shamans of the Native American tribes and root doctors differ in their approach to magick and spiritual healing. Shamans don't need to call out the spirit of a plant, as they believe it is already there and active.

Psychic reading is another essential tool in the root doctor's skill set. These readings not only identify which spirits are involved in the client's life but also advise the healer on which treatments may work best. For example, a treatment can be as simple as preparing a ritual bath and prescribing psalms and prayers to fix the situation, or more in-depth work involving candles and vigils with repeated prayers and petitions over the course of several days may be required. Because of this ability to see and hear spirits while working and healing in the physical world, many root doctors are called "two-headed."

TROLLDOM AND TROLLKUNNING

Root doctors are not the only folk and holistic healers who perform readings to understand the reason behind a client's symptoms. The practice of trolldom (also spelled trolddom) is an ancient Norse folk-magick tradition once performed throughout Scandinavia by practitioners known as *trollkunnings*. Many refer to trolldom as Norse hoodoo.

Trolldom practitioners would often work together on issues within a community. One would do readings, one would do physical healing work, and another would focus on magickal spells and spiritual practices. Trollkunnings also dealt with nature spirits, particularly ones known as the Hidden People, or elves. Norse folk had a fear of being "elf shot," or struck by the unseen arrows of elves, which would cause pain and agony in the victim. Specific plants and spells were used to prevent these attacks or to cure the pain after someone had been shot.

Today there are not as many trolldom practitioners left, so many of those who remain are adept in all areas of this practice.

Like many other healing methods, working with spirits is very important in trolldom, and there are some specific spirits that are unique to these traditions and practices. As in rootwork, several Christian elements are involved in the tradition as well. Interestingly, there are more recorded spells in trolldom calling on Jesus, God, Mary, and the Devil than there are ones calling on Odin or other deities found in Norse and Pagan traditions. The reason for this is simple: trolldom is the magick of the people, and like people, the practices changed and evolved with the times. When Christianity became the dominant religion in the region, the practice simply added elements of those beliefs into an already firmly ensconced tradition.

A major difference in the practice of trolldom is that, unlike shamanism and root doctoring, it's appropriate to call upon the Devil to fix your problems . . . as long as he is the *cause* of them. It is believed that Satan isn't really a free being but is under the control of Jesus and God and is powerless against God's orders. Therefore, if you command Satan out of your life in God's name, he has to leave you alone. In the same vein, a believer can command the Devil to control his minions or any dark spirits that are causing mischief and spiritual ailments.

CALLING ON YOUR GOD(S)

Prayer is a very powerful practice that provides direct communication between spirits and common folk. Most everyone knows how to pray. There are some traditional Christian prayers—for example, Hail Mary, Our Father, and Psalm 23—that many people know and recite, but there are also spontaneous prayers that are said in the moment, and they have power in them as well. It's your connection to your higher power that is most important.

Giving thanks to your god or higher power is always a nice way to start off any prayer. Expressing gratitude for what we already have raises our own energetic vibrations, which in turn determines the way we request help. (Imagine the difference between telling your higher power that everything is awful, so you need him or her to make it all better, as opposed to saying "Thank you so much for all that I have and all the beauty in my life. Please, I could use some help with my health these days. . . .") We always catch more flies with honey, even on the spiritual plane!

Trance work is also a common practice for calling on deities in many traditions. These out-of-body states allow practitioners to see spirits and work with them in a more direct manner than prayer allows.

The use of herbs and herbal treatments is also very common among different practices. While a variety of different herbs may be used for the same type of treatments, the intention is always to call on their unique energies as well as nature itself to fix the specified problems and help the recipient live a good life. (You can read more about this in the sections on medicine men and women and root doctors in this chapter.)

REIKI

Reiki is one of the most popular forms of
healing by touch (or almost touch, as the
hands don't actually need to make contact to
be an effective corrective source). Developed
in the 1920s by Mikao Usui, a Japanese
Buddhist, the practice is especially useful in
the fact that practitioners can use it not only
to heal others but also to heal themselves.

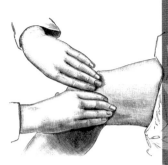

Reiki is based on the principle that each of us contains an invisible
life force, or *qi*, that rules our emotions and physical well-being. When
that force runs low, we're more likely to feel "off." Reiki practitioners work
to restore balance by bringing the life force back up to an optimal level.

The basic concept of Western Reiki involves positioning the
hands in specific ways just above or on the body. A full treatment can
last for thirty minutes to an hour. Spot treatments can be used when a
person has a specific area they are interested in healing. During a spot
treatment, the Reiki worker will place their hands over the area where
there are issues, or they will simply place their hands on the shoulders.
Theory holds that Reiki energy is so in tune with the body that it will
seek out and heal physical, emotional, and spiritual wounds even if the
practitioner's hands aren't directly over the source of the pain. Many
Reiki masters can send healing long distance, via telephone or video calls!

One unique aspect of Reiki is that practitioners are expected to
adhere to a set of guidelines for living mindfully and in the moment.
The main principles are as follows:

Just for today I will let go of worry.
Just for today I will let go of anger.
Just for today I will give thanks for my many blessings.
Just for today I will do my work honestly.

There are different forms of Reiki and different levels of practice. To evolve to the highest level, an established master passes the power to heal to a student through a method called *attunement*. The best way to learn Reiki is to find a local attuned master teacher.

Hands-on Healing

The laying-on of hands has been around for thousands of years, since well before the birth of Christ, who himself performed miracles of healing with just a simple touch. In fact, the Catholic Church to this day canonizes saints based on how many miracles he or she performed while alive, and many of these include healing by hand. While faith healing is usually associated with a religion of some sort, if you are interested in learning more about hands-on healing techniques, there are plenty of nondenominational methods of moving energy through the body to affect a healthy outcome, including integrated energy therapy (IET), polarity therapy, qigong, Quantum-Touch®, pranic healing, and Healing Touch™.

Self-Healing Ritual

Before you can heal others, it is important to heal yourself. The following energy-healing ritual allows you to gather healing energy from the universe and direct it at yourself.

Materials

White sage smudge stick

Healing incense

Sharp knife

Blue candle

Relaxing music

Ritual

Take the smudge stick and cleanse the room in which you are about to do your healing work. Focus on the room being filled with a white light. Light the incense.Use the knife to inscribe the words "health and wellness" on the candle. Light the candle and turn on the music. Sit in a comfortable position. Rub your hands together. Focus on the feeling of being healed and completely whole. Have that energy fill up the space between your hands. Once you feel your hands glowing, run them over your body, starting with your head and going down to your feet.

When you feel you have received energy throughout your body, shake the excess energy off your hands. Snuff out the candle and incense and shut off the music. Go about your day feeling healed and complete.

MEDITATION
GET INTO THE SPIRIT

In order to access the parts of the mind where kindness, compassion, and mysticism live, we need to shed a few things—namely judgment, anxiety, and racing thoughts. Meditation is a great way to begin this process and find our spiritual selves.

Meditation is a practice that is as old as humankind and is known in some form in every corner of the world. Thirty or forty years ago in the United States, meditation was something that the average person knew very little about, believing that it was an odd form of transcendence used only by Buddhists or hippies. Nowadays, of course, meditation is practiced by all kinds of folks—old, young, male, female, professionals, and, yes, hippies, too.

Simply put, meditation is a state of mind where you focus your energy inward, to the point where everything else falls away and you're left with your truest, purest self. In other words, you put all the worries of your day-to-day life aside and get down to who you are without all the baggage that weighs you down—the job, the kids, the arguments with your friends, your finances. None of those things define who you truly are. We tend to forget that once upon a time we came into this world with a joyful heart, curiosity about everything, and a willingness to listen to our instincts. Those are the things that meditation can give back to you.

If you are interested in meditation, here are some basic guidelines for beginning a meditation practice: take a minute and think about the stressors in your life, the things that are eclipsing your truest self. Think about the roles you have fallen into—again, perhaps not by choice but merely because they were default options. Write them down. You're going to work on letting go of the roles that don't serve your highest self and replace them with the positive energy of your true spirituality and being.

Start by Getting Comfortable

Simplicity is the key to avoiding distraction, especially when you're in search of your true being. To begin, find or make a space that is tranquil. Think of wherever you are as a sacred space. You may be sitting in your bedroom, but you're entering the inner sanctum of your mind. What will help you relax so you can focus on your work here? Soft music? Incense? White noise? Candles? Chimes? Go all out if you want—the whole practice is ethereal, leading you back to the self that's always been there but has been lost under a bunch of modern-day distractions. Prepare your space for this special homecoming.

When you're beginning this journey of the self, make yourself as comfortable as possible. The most common way to meditate is by sitting in a comfortable seat with your legs uncrossed and flat on the floor. If you are not prone to falling asleep at the drop of a hat, you can try lying on a mat on the floor. Again, you're trying to eliminate any issues of discomfort that would distract you from focusing on your practice, which is why you should begin your practice with an easy posture that allows you to relax and focus.

When you're comfortable, simply start by taking deep breaths, in and out. And by "deep," I don't mean inhaling just a tad deeper than usual—I mean inhale so deeply that your chest fills and rises. Hold it a second and then blow the breath out completely. Inhale through your nose; exhale through your mouth. Think of your inhalation as bringing in good energy and your exhalation as ridding yourself of anxiety, anger, bitterness, and other negative emotions.

Give yourself time to just listen to your own breathing and to the sounds around you. Let yourself experience what it feels like to let go of unhelpful emotions and energy. Just *be* in this moment. Tell yourself "There is no past, there is no future, there is only now." This mantra serves to remind you that there is no use worrying about what happened yesterday, because it's done. There's no use worrying about tomorrow, because tomorrow will "take care of itself," as they say. All any of us knows for sure is in the current moment. This concept, although simple, is *big*, and it's vital in learning to let go of emotional baggage.

The purpose of meditation is not to completely clear the mind but to let go of worry and anxiety while allowing yourself to deeply relax. If you find yourself thinking about an issue that brings up negative feelings, just let it go without judgment. When meditation becomes a regular part of your life, you will find that you are able to accept each moment of your day—even the stressful times—in a calm, even-keeled manner, because you have learned to push judgment (of other people, of situations, and, just as importantly, of yourself) aside.

This is what we refer to as *mindfulness*: being fully aware of our present surroundings without attaching any thought or judgment to them. When we master mindfulness, we know there's no use worrying about what's already happened or what we believe could happen. There are a lot of things that we don't know and we don't have control over, and we are okay with that. We let life happen at its own pace, without trying to dictate its outcomes. And when we can give up the power that we think we have over life, there is great peace.

Aim for several minutes of meditation several days a week when you first begin. As you become more comfortable with the process, you can lengthen the duration of your practice and make it part of your daily routine.

Reach for a Higher Level

You may be thinking "How can I stop judging thoughts and events? I can't help myself!" That's true. As fallible humans, the vast majority of us judge things so quickly that we often don't even realize we are doing it. The point of meditation—and one of its long-term benefits—is to recognize when those judgments are creeping into our unconsciousness, taking root, and shaping our lives in a negative way.

The philosopher Friedrich Nietzsche said, "There are no eternal facts, as there are no absolute truths." What this means is that what may be "true" to one person isn't necessarily true for everyone else. For example, you might think your neighbor is a loud, inconsiderate jerk. Other people in your building might know that your neighbor is deaf and plays his television at top volume because he can't hear it. Where you have contempt for him, others may have compassion—you're all just interpreting the situation through the facts available to you at the time. The problem is, sometimes we don't have all the facts before we form those opinions—and furthermore, we don't question what we think we know.

Meditation helps you to slow down, to think before you act and form opinions, and to accept things as they are and nothing more. Think of it as one way to wipe the slate clean (or as clean as possible) on a regular basis—to look your fears and opinions right in the eye and question whether they're absolute truth.

With a clear mind and a clear conscience, you open the door to allowing yourself to see everything in a completely new way—perhaps even the way that the angels among us view the world.

USING SPIRITUALITY EVERY DAY

It's not enough for us to simply find the path that makes us the best that we can be. (You knew it couldn't be that easy, right?) What's important is for us to practice what we preach. Not in the sense that you need to recruit legions of men and women to your personal spiritual practice, but in the sense that what brings you peace during your quiet meditation session should also be the thing that you can call on to bring you peace in moments of stress.

No matter how much we work at finding our own inner peace, we'll always have to deal with people who are not on a spiritual path and seem hell-bent on destroying themselves and/or anyone in their way. Interactions with these kinds of people are all opportunities for spiritual growth, believe it or not. When you're faced with someone who is rude, aggressive, or just plain mean, it's a time for you to dig deep (sometimes *really* deep) to react to them with as much love and understanding as you can muster.

For instance, imagine that you are standing in line waiting for your morning coffee when a stranger butts in front of you. You have a choice here, and you can react in several ways. You can yell at the person and say "Hey, jerk, get to the back of the line!" You can get physically aggressive and remove the person from the line. You can approach the person calmly and rationally. Or you could choose to do nothing at all.

This is a time for mindfulness, for calling on your higher powers and asking what they might do in the same situation. Nastiness and physical aggression rarely solve issues in the long run, nor do they change minds. Likewise, standing by and doing nothing isn't always the best answer, as it promotes an environment in which bullies get away with pushing around peaceful men and women. Finding the rational, peace-loving voice inside of you may be difficult, but it's something you can practice and learn to use in the real world. In this example, you might say to the line jumper "We've all been waiting, and everyone's time is valuable. It's disrespectful for you to ignore the rest of us who have been here longer." Those are just the neutral facts of the matter, delivered (hopefully) without aggression. If the line cutter doesn't respond by going to the end of the line, you may have at least inspired others to take action in the future and to use a rational, peaceful mode of communication when they find themselves irritated by someone else.

Line jumping is annoying, but it's generally a short-lived event—a mere blip on your daily radar. What about dealing with a boss, spouse, or other family member who is making your life miserable? There's no easy escape here. There are personal and even legal entanglements involved, and you want to do what's best for yourself and also those around you. The principles remain the same as the line-jumping example: reach as far down as you can to pull out reason, love, and empathy. You don't need to pound the other person over the head with platitudes about peace and cooperation; you can simply refuse to engage in hostile conversations and inform the other person that you are willing to talk at a later time, when emotions are not running high.

The rub is this: someone who is unenlightened enough to intentionally act in a callous or hurtful manner may tell you to put your nonhostility where the sun doesn't shine. But that's okay, because you're still making yourself heard and setting an example for others. None of this is to say that you should let others take advantage of you—it's simply a reminder that when your spirit is solid and you feel at peace with yourself and your decisions, you can stand strong in any situation.

Sweetening Spell

Sometimes even when you are calm and collected, key people in your life, such as your boss or life partner, still will not listen to you. This invariably makes you upset, causing you to have further issues communicating your desires. At times a little magickal touch may be in order. Try the following conjure spell to open up their minds and let them understand your point of view.

Materials

Pen and paper

Small jar

For a boss: a business card with their name on it

For your partner: a photograph of the person

2 teaspoons dried lavender

2 teaspoons dried master of the woods/woodruff

2 teaspoons dried ginkgo leaf

Mortar and pestle

Sugar

Photograph of yourself

1 rubber band

3 tea-light candles

Ritual

On the paper, write out your petition and desire for change (be as specific as you can for the exact need at hand). Include any and all details about what you are trying to get across. Place the petition in the jar.

Add the business card or photo of the person to the jar. Next, take the lavender, master of the woods, and ginkgo leaf and grind them into a fine powder. Add the sugar and mix thoroughly. Sprinkle the herbal mixture into the jar and seal it. Take the photo of you and position it on the outside of the jar. Place the rubber band around the photo and jar so that your photo is facing outward.

With your pen, inscribe on each candle one of the following: "Understanding," "Listening," "Open Mind." Light the candles. Hold the jar over the candles and shake it. As you shake the jar, chant:

"Thinking sweetly from afar / Open the mind in this jar."

Continue to shake the jar twice a day for a week, reciting the chant until your target listens to you and what you have to say.

Freeze and Sweeten Spell

People who are unable to hit the pause button on offensive or irritating behavior even when asked nicely may need a little help to "freeze" them in their tracks so they can reconsider their actions. This simple freezer spell will help you to deal with those situations.

Materials

Scissors

Pen and paper

Ice cube tray

2 teaspoons sugar

2 teaspoons dried lavender

Water

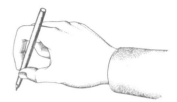

Ritual

Cut the paper into small slips so you have as many slips of paper as there are cavities in your ice cube tray. On each slip, write the name of the person who will not stop giving you or your loved ones a hard time. Place a slip of paper into each cavity of the ice cube tray. Add a pinch of sugar and lavender to each cavity in the tray. Fill the tray with water. As you fill the tray with water, chant:

"Frozen will you be 'til your actions sweeter be."

Let the tray freeze for a week. After a week, once a day take one ice cube from the tray and let it melt in a glass or bowl. Once the ice has melted, pour the water onto the earth at the base of a tree or at a crossroads, sending the sweetened thoughts and actions to the person and the universe.

In the end, what's important to know about dealing with unenlightened men and women is that nothing they do is personal. It may feel *very* personal at the time, but someone who deals in aggression, backstabbing, deceit, or similar behaviors has some ugly demons they are fighting—and the demons are winning. These are not people whom we should fear; these folks deserve our empathy. Once you start viewing them in this light, you may have an easier time reacting to them in a way that doesn't invoke hatred but, rather, compassion for what they don't know about having peace in their own lives.

Healing Light Spell

Sometimes we want to try to heal the world and offer peace and hope. This simple spell can help us send light, love, hope, and healing to the world at large.

Materials

> Sharp knife
>
> Pink candle
>
> 2 teaspoons dried lavender
>
> 2 teaspoons dried catnip
>
> 2 teaspoons dried ginkgo leaf
>
> World map

Ritual

Use the knife to inscribe the words "Love, Peace, and Light" on the pink candle.

Mix the lavender, catnip, and ginkgo leaf together. Lay the world map across your altar or work surface. Sprinkle the herbal mixture across the map (be sure that a little bit of the powder lands on every continent). Light the pink candle and place it on the center of the map. As the candle burns, envision a pink light enveloping the earth.

Recite the chant:

"Pretty, pink, peaceful light
Envelop the world on this night."

Let the candle burn down. Once the candle has burned completely, bury the remains of the candle and the herbs at a crossroads to send the light and peace into the earth and through the earth to all of humanity.

WE'RE ALL IN THIS TOGETHER

With all of this talk about spirituality and ways to achieve your highest self, you might be wondering where to begin, especially if this is all new to you. It's easy to get confused by the different branches of spirituality, the possibilities, and the ideas that are out there. You can begin just by seeking out the best in yourself and in others.

All of life comes down to the choices we make every day. We can choose to have a positive or negative outlook. Following that logic, we can choose to be a positive or negative force in society. Gandhi urged his followers to "Be the change you wish to see in the world"—a simple yet very powerful message. We can choose to lead not by words but by example, even in the worst of times.

This isn't so much about a set of beliefs as it is about honoring all of our fellow beings and opening our minds and hearts to their journeys alongside us on this earth. Here are some simple ways to raise the energetic vibration in your life.

LOOK FOR WAYS TO HELP OTHERS. It doesn't have to be as big as building someone a house. It can be something simple, like dropping by an elderly neighbor to make sure they're all right or just to give them some company. It can be listening to a child instead of shrugging them off. Take a look around you. Chances are high that there are people you see every day who could use a helping hand.

CUT THE GOSSIP. Gossip, although very satisfying when the subject of the story is someone who's hurt you in the past, creates negative energy. This is a tough one for many of us, because we often gossip without thinking. Try to make an effort over the next week to not engage in gossip and see how it feels.

BE KIND. This sounds simple, but kindness is something we often let slide, especially when we're busy and stressed out. We blame others for things that aren't really their fault. (Is it really the slow driver's fault that you're going to be late for work when you're the one who overslept?) We tend to focus only on our own stories, without acknowledging that everyone we see has their own problems. Give your positive energy to others when you can. You'll be surprised at how often it comes back to you.

BE MINDFUL. Don't attach judgment to people, ideas, or events. The past is gone; the future will happen as it's supposed to. The only certainty any of us has is the moment we're in.

REMEMBER: WE ARE ALL ONE. What you do to me affects you; what I do to you affects me. And so it goes. None of us lives in a vacuum. There are no isolated incidents. Cruelty is as contagious as love; choose love whenever you can.

KNOW THAT NOTHING IS PERSONAL. As we discussed earlier, you're going to meet some people on your path who are less than kind and who have no interest in achieving spiritual awareness. As awful as they may be, remember that nothing they do is personal. Imagine that you are a light bulb and every time you feel at peace, you shine a little brighter and feel a little warmer. Now imagine someone who has no peace and whose bulb is dark and cold all the time. You might behave badly, too, if you felt that way. Keeping this in mind will help you from being pulled into the muck of unenlightened beings and losing faith in your own spiritual path.

ACT WITH LOVE, ALWAYS. The one emotion you should strive for in your day-to-day dealings is love. Hostility, anger, and hatred are all destructive emotions, and even though we may think they can be the most effective way to get things done—"Just do it the way I said, or I'll make sure you get fired!"—there are better ways to work together. When we approach people and situations with love, the energy is completely different. It's doing something because you want to, not because you're afraid of what will happen if you don't.

USE THE PLATINUM RULE. For centuries, we've been told that we should treat others the way we want to be treated. You know what's even better? Treating others the way *they* want to be treated. This takes great awareness and empathy, but it's absolutely priceless to the other person.

Perhaps the most important thing you can do as a beginner on your spiritual journey is to find a practice or a philosophy that truly speaks to you. Does it feel right? Do you really "get" the beliefs or teachings? Are you inspired by it? Spirituality should be a light part of our beings, and our practice shouldn't feel forced. It should bring joy and peace into the day and be something that you look forward to engaging in—it should not feel like a heavy-handed obligation.

In other words, what works for your friends, your family, or your parents may not be the spiritual path that sets you on your way to ultimate wisdom, and that's all right. There is no one truth. There are many different mindsets and ways to achieve your highest self. So explore, and when you find something that feels good to you, work it into your daily practice, and have fun with it. Remember that your spirit is meant to soar!

Keep the Wildlife Healthy and Well

Witches often cast spells to encourage good health and well-being not only for themselves and their families, but also for the living creatures in our environment. If our pets get sick, we can take them along to the local veterinarian, but our local wildlife is not so lucky. Witches feel it is important to do their bit and try their best to keep every living thing happy and healthy. If you would like to magickally participate in helping your environment and protecting wildlife from illness and disease, take a walk in the woods and collect a large bag of acorns. Acorns are considered to hold the properties of protection and good fortune, and when collected in numbers of twenty or more, will produce a powerful barrier to ward off negativity. If it's the wrong time of year, it's quite all right to source the acorns from the Internet.

Take a few small twigs from the woodland to represent nature and gather some nearby leaves. Place all these woodland treasures into a drawstring bag. When you're back at home, set up an altar and lay out the items as follows:

Scatter some sea salt onto the table to purify the space, then place three green candles in the center and light them.

Situate the pouch in front of the candles and say this spell:

"Spirits of nature, the magick you weave,
Bring power to this spell with these acorns and leaves,
All of the creatures are healthy and free,
Bring total protection to all that we see."

Let the candles burn all the way down, and then gather up the salt and place it inside the pouch. On the next full moon, return to the woodland where you gathered your items and scatter them back on the ground. This magick will ensure that everything stays in balance. The animals and insects will remain healthy and be protected forever.

Part Three

CRAFT YOUR OWN PERSONAL MAGICK

DIY
Brews and
Potions

NATURE'S
SUPERHEROES

THE WITCHES' BREW
POTIONS—LIQUID SPELLS

One of the most romanticized views of witchcraft from olden times is of a witch standing over an open fire, stirring up potions in a cauldron. Today, witches still brew all sorts of potions for love, luck, health, wealth, and much more. The only real differences are in the materials: a kitchen stove is used instead of an open fire, and a stainless-steel pot—or kettle, depending on the potion being made—often replaces the cauldron.

Potions are widely regarded as one of the main instruments in a witch's tool kit. Potions are simply liquid spells taken internally or applied externally. These spells come in a variety of forms, from enchanted perfumes to teas, tinctures, and washes. Some potions are used in ritual or magickal work, and some potions are used for healing work.

Potions are great examples of just how practical kitchen witchcraft (see chapter 8) can be.

PRACTICAL HOLISTIC HEALTH
KITCHEN HERBS AND COMMON PLANTS FOR BREWS

There was a time when homemade teas and salves were the only medicines available to people. Many of these folk remedies still have validity in the modern world. Today more and more people are looking into home remedies and holistic health rather than just over-the-counter remedies bought in any store. This holistic approach to health that treats the mind, body, and soul together is often both effective and practical. Holistic health does not need to be about expensive, organic brands or high-end oils. You can utilize what you already have at home to your advantage.

Take a look at what you have in your kitchen cabinet. You will likely find things like cayenne pepper, basil, thyme, rosemary, oregano, cinnamon, allspice, parsley, and mustard seed. These herbs and spices, as well as onion, garlic, and ginger, all have some sort of medicinal value.

Take a look in your backyard. You may see pine or birch trees, dandelions, goldenrods, plantains, or nettles. You may have elderberries, blueberries, blackberries, or raspberries. These plants are often easy to find and identify, making them practical for homegrown homeopathic remedies. (Of course, if you do not have these types of plants in your yard, or if you live in a city, you can easily find most of them in some form or another online or at the market.)

You can use many of these plants to make tinctures, teas, and decoctions. You can also make syrups, tonics, waters, and vinegars. By working with the herbs that you have on hand, you can create your own remedies with a distinct local flavor.

The Power Behind the Plants

Witches believe that many spiritual forces animate the world. This belief is called animism. When a witch works with a plant or crystal or performs a spell or ritual at a specific location, they are working with the spirits behind those plants or crystals and calling upon the spirit of that location to aid them in their work. The witch and spirits form spiritual partnerships and alliances; these can manifest in the form of animals (witch's familiars), or in the form of other plants, crystals, and locations. Through working with these spirits over time and on various projects, the relationships deepen and develop. The witches gain information on magical associations, properties, and lore, often through dreams, inspirations, or visions. The spirits gain energy, attention, and, often, physical shelter—as animals or plants in a home or garden, or as a crystal being carried as a talisman.

Giving an offering of prayer to the plant spirits of the ingredients we will use in this chapter's remedies is a way of honoring them for providing their help. We are acknowledging them as our allies and asking them to assist us.

Praying also empowers potions with power for magickal work and healing. Prayer is a powerful tool for holistic health, as it can unite the mind, body, and spirit. It is the most powerful tool we have to cultivate a

THANK YOU PRAYER TO PLANT ALLIES

"To the spirit of (insert plant name here), I thank you for your sacrifice. Thank you for giving yourself to me to sustain me, heal me, help me, and protect me. May your essence fill me with health, and may your blessings fall upon me. Spirit of (insert plant name here), may you be blessed. Thank you for your sacrifice."

connection with the spirit world, including our own inner spirit. Prayer activates our own spirit forces to work in tandem with the plant spirits and the plant's natural healing attributes.

The following prayer is a guide to get you started. It should be recited before making any of the recipes in this chapter. If you are working with multiple herbs, you can name them all at once or perform the prayer for each herb individually. Once you start working with plant spirits and energy, you will discover your own prayer to say to them, and

there may happen to be a different prayer for each plant ally you have.

Say the prayer with your eyes closed, standing with your hands over the herbs, palms down. One hand is there to receive their energy, and one hand is there to direct your energy to them. Hold this position for a few moments and visualize the spirit energy of the plant reacting to your spirit energy. See the plant's spirit energy rise up through one hand and your spirit reach down through the other. This will seal the connection between the two of you.

TEAS AND DECOCTIONS FOR HEALTH

One of the easiest ways to work with homeopathic remedies is through the use of teas and *decoctions*: herb-and-water remedies in the form of concocted potions that you drink.

Teas and decoctions (as well as tinctures, discussed below) made with dried herbs, roots, or flowers are all *infusions*: herbs soaked in water, which transfers the properties of the herbs into the liquid.

The cold-infusion method is used for *tinctures*, where the herbal properties are absorbed and released into liquids over time. Hot infusions are used for teas and decoctions, where herbal properties are released into the liquid through heat and cooking.

A decoction is typically made with the woody and seedy plant parts, such as roots and bark. Once the plant parts are boiled in the liquid, they are then placed on a low heat and set to simmer for fifteen to twenty minutes (the sturdier the plant matter, the longer it needs to simmer). After the herbs have simmered, cool them and then strain and press the herbs through cheesecloth or a strainer. The mixture is then ready to drink. For teas, the flowers, leaves, fruits, and/or stems of plants are typically used. It is preferred to start steeping the herbs in the water before it reaches a full boil, but you can also wait until the water boils.

Once the water begins to steam or boil, remove it from the heat. Steep teas for no more than five to ten minutes. Then, while still hot, strain into a container. You can drink the tea right away, or, if you prefer iced tea, pour the strained liquid into a container and place in the fridge for thirty minutes to an hour.

As mentioned previously, you can work with dried herbs or fresh herbs directly if they are available, but some of the herbs discussed in this chapter—such as peppermint and chamomile—are readily available in herbal tea bags at the market, ready to use. This is a perfectly acceptable way to work with these teas.

Herbs for Teas and Decoctions

The following list includes the most popular herbs and spices and the health issues they can help address. All you need to make the tea or decoction is a kettle or pot to boil the water in and something to contain the spices or plant components for steeping. If you are using a tea ball, use only a pinch of each plant or spice. If you are using an infusion pot or something similar, you can use approximately ¼ teaspoon of each ingredient. Again, the herbs should be used for either teas or decoctions depending on the plant materials used. If you are using the root, seeds, or bark, use the decoction method. If you are using the flowers, leaves, fruits, or stem, use the tea method. If you use a combination of plant matter, use the decoction method but then drink it iced (following the cold tea method).

ANGELICA ROOT Soothes colds and flu, reduces phlegm and fever; expectorant (do *not* use if you are diabetic)

BASIL Eases headaches, indigestion, muscle spasms, insomnia, earaches; reduces stress and tension, improves skin

BLACKBERRY (leaves or roots) Reduces diarrhea (*note: blackberry roots are used as a decoction, while blackberry leaves are used for tea*)

CATNIP Soothes teething pain, colic, diarrhea, indigestion, anxiety, insomnia (may cause drowsiness, avoid if on lithium or sedatives)

CALENDULA (marigold) Reduces fevers and diarrhea; soothes indigestion, gastrointestinal cramps, flu; antiseptic (may cause drowsiness, avoid if on sedatives)

CAYENNE PEPPER Soothes coughs, colds, arthritis, nerve pain, fever, flu; expectorant (avoid taking with medications that slow blood-clotting and with theophylline)

CHAMOMILE Reduces insomnia, anxiety, stress, fever, arthritis, indigestion; aids with sleep and pain relief (may decrease effectiveness of birth-control pills and some cancer medications, and may increase the effects of warfarin; discuss usage with your doctor if you are taking medication for your liver)

CINNAMON BARK Soothes sore throats and coughs, anti-inflammatory (avoid taking with diabetes medications)

DANDELION ROOT Detoxifying, aids digestion, relieves constipation, laxative (avoid if on antibiotics, lithium, or water pills)

DANDELION LEAF Mild diuretic, potassium rich (discuss usage with your doctor if you are taking medication for your liver)

ELDERBERRY BERRY Wards off colds and flu

ELDERBERRY FLOWER Reduces fever (avoid taking with medications that decrease the immune system)

GARLIC (for syrups) Antiseptic, eases atherosclerosis, rheumatism, ear infections, urinary tract infections; supports healthy cholesterol; helps lower blood pressure; boosts immune system; expectorant; reduces risks of colon, rectal, and prostate cancers (do *not* take with isoniazid or medications used for HIV/AIDS, or with medications used to slow blood-clotting)

GINGER Eases morning sickness, nausea, colic, indigestion, diarrhea, fever, sore throats (avoid taking with medications that slow blood-clotting)

GINKGO Relieves anxiety, vertigo, tinnitus; improves circulation, helps concentration; helps vision and premenstrual syndrome (avoid taking with ibuprofen or with medications that slow blood clotting; numerous medications have interactions with ginkgo; discuss usage with your health-care practitioner before taking)

GINSENG Aphrodisiac, mild stimulant, boosts the immune system (do *not* take with medications that slow blood-clotting, and avoid taking with diabetes medications or with MAO inhibitors)

GOLDENROD Relieves gout and cramps

LAVENDER Relieves anxiety, headaches, tension, stress, indigestion, irritable bowel syndrome; antibacterial; antiseptic; disinfectant (may cause drowsiness, avoid if on sedatives)

LEMON BALM Relieves anxiety, cold sores, colic, insomnia, restlessness, indigestion; boosts memory (may cause drowsiness, avoid taking with sedatives)

NETTLE Relieves hay fever and arthritis; diuretic (avoid taking with diabetes medications, medications for high blood pressure, sedatives, medications that slow blood-clotting, and lithium)

ONION (for syrups) Helps lower systolic blood pressure, relieves colds, antiseptic (avoid taking with medications that slow blood clotting)

PARSLEY Helps with iron deficiency, anemia, fatigue; diuretic (do *not* take with medications that slow blood-clotting or with diuretics)

PEPPERMINT Relieves nausea, anxiety, indigestion, irritable bowel syndrome, colic, diarrhea, fever, coughs, colds; anesthetic (avoid if you have acid-reflux disease; avoid taking with cyclosporine; discuss usage with your doctor if you are taking any medications that are changed by the liver)

PINE NEEDLES Expectorant; antiseptic; relieves coughs, colds, fever, congestion

ROSEMARY Improves focus, memory, concentration, blood pressure, circulation; antiseptic, antidepressant; eases indigestion

THYME Antibacterial, antiseptic, eases coughs and colds, expectorant (do *not* take with medications that slow blood-clotting)

This is just a small list of the many herbs that can be made into teas or decoctions. Each of these herbs can be used individually in a single herbal tea or be combined with others to create a variety of herbal teas.

Tea and Decoction Health Blends

Now that you have a list of herbs to work from, it's time to look at herbal tea blends for your different health needs.

Important note: The amounts listed here are for dried herbs, flowers, and spices. Dried ingredients are preferred for teas. If you wish to use fresh ingredients for decoctions, and they are available, double the amount. See cautions and interactions in the herb list on pages 198–200.

Anxiety Relief

- ¼ teaspoon chamomile
- ¼ teaspoon lemon balm

Mood Booster

- ¼ teaspoon lavender
- ¼ teaspoon catnip
- ¼ teaspoon rosemary

Arthritis/Joint Pain

- ¼ teaspoon goldenrod
- ¼ teaspoon ground cayenne pepper
  Note: after the tea cools, apply it by rubbing the liquid into the affected area.

Circulation

- ¼ teaspoon ginkgo leaf
- ¼ teaspoon ginger
- ¼ teaspoon rosemary

Cold Relief

- ¼ teaspoon elderberry flower
- ¼ teaspoon thyme

Gastrointestinal Cramp Relief

- ¼ teaspoon basil
- ¼ teaspoon calendula (marigold)
- ¼ teaspoon goldenrod

Diarrhea Relief

- ¼ teaspoon blackberry root
- ¼ teaspoon catnip

Energizing Tea

- ¼ teaspoon ginseng
- ¼ teaspoon peppermint

Expectorant

- 1/4 teaspoon pine needles
- 1/4 teaspoon nettle leaf
- 1/4 teaspoon angelica root

Fatigue Relief

- 1/4 teaspoon ginseng
- 1/4 teaspoon lemon balm

Fever Break

- 1/8 teaspoon cayenne pepper
- 1/4 teaspoon angelica root

Flu Relief

- 1/4 teaspoon calendula (marigold)
- 1/4 teaspoon lemon balm

Headache Relief

- 1/4 teaspoon basil
- 1/4 teaspoon thyme
- 1/4 teaspoon lavender

Immune-System Booster

- 1/2 teaspoon dried elderberries
- 1/4 teaspoon nettle
- 1/4 teaspoon calendula (marigold)

Indigestion Relief

- 1/2 teaspoon ginger
- 1/4 teaspoon lemon balm
- 1/4 teaspoon peppermint

Sleepy Time

- 1/2 teaspoon chamomile
- 1/4 teaspoon catnip
- 1/4 teaspoon lavender

Sore Throat Relief

- 1/8 teaspoon cinnamon
- 1/8 teaspoon ginger
  Note: add honey after steeped

Stress Relief

- 1/4 teaspoon basil
- 1/4 teaspoon chamomile
- 1/4 teaspoon lavender
- 1/4 teaspoon peppermint

Cleansing

- 1/4 teaspoon dandelion leaf
- 1/8 teaspoon goldenrod
- 1/8 teaspoon parsley

MAGICKAL TEAS

By working with holistic potions for health and wellness, you can bring magick into your body as well as into your daily life.

Many of the same herbs we use for health can also be used for practical magick and spiritual workings. Magick does not have to be fancy, nor does it require expensive herbs from exotic locations. The most effective magick uses what you have available to you locally. Any magickal working can be done with the herbs found in your kitchen spice cabinet or by walking in the woods.

Holistic health deals with the health of the spirit as well. Magick taps into our spirit to manifest changes in the world. It is through working with the magickal and spiritual associations of herbs that we can truly obtain holistic health and balance the mind, body, and spirit.

Making magickal teas follows the same process as making teas for healing (see pages 196–197). The magick is brought in through your intent, which is directed through incantations, prayers, and, occasionally, envisioning colored lights. The prayers and incantations provide directions for the plant spirits, which work with your spirit to bring about the desired changes.

Working with teas in magick is a form of *kitchen magick* or *kitchen witchcraft* (see chapter 8, page 238). By drinking magick teas, you are taking the magick inside your body. This form of magick reflects the alchemical axiom "as above, so below; as within, so without." By taking the magick inside yourself, you will start to see changes outside yourself.

Healing Magick Teas

All the herbal blends for teas, decoctions, and syrups mentioned thus far in this chapter can also be used in a magickal fashion. Just take the recipe, look up the corresponding magickal attributes in the list on pages 206–207, and follow these extra steps:

Step 1:

As you steep the potion, envision yourself covered in either a blue or green light (whichever color represents healing to you).

Step 2:

As you drink the potion, visualize a blue or green light coming from the liquid. Once you drink it, the light will start radiating from within throughout your whole body and then out into the world around you. See it reach to heaven (as above) and into the earth (so below), extending your will and desire into the universe.

If you are the kind of person who likes affirmations and chants, try this one:

"Herbs grown naturally,
Health and wellness come to me."

The simple use of an affirmation when intent and emotion are added makes an action magickal. By preparing the teas with the intent to be healed and adding emotional forces to the mixture, the act of drinking the tea will release and direct the energy within, creating internal and powerful magick.

Herbs for Magickal Teas

All of the herbs used in the medicinal teas on pages 201–202 also have magickal and spiritual attributes—these attributes are listed here. As you work with the plant spirits, you will start to learn which of the plant's properties are most important to you. For example, Charity worked a lot with marigold for healing and psychic development before the marigold spirit encouraged her to work with it in money spells. She soon started to have success in money work involving marigold. Let the spirits guide you and your powers will grow every day.

ANGELICA ROOT Angel work, protection, hex removal, exorcisms, health, meditation, divination (do *not* use if you are diabetic)

BASIL Love, exorcisms, wealth, astral travel, rituals for the dead, house blessings, ancestral work, calling on and working with dragon spirits, calling draconic or dragon spirit–based energy into your spell, protection, attracting money

BLACKBERRY Healing, money, protection, exorcism

CATNIP Love, beauty, happiness, calling on the energy of cats, working with cat spirits, used as an offering for cat spirits, breaking spells, fertility, psychic powers (may cause drowsiness, avoid if on lithium or sedatives)

CALENDULA (marigold) Money, prosperity, health, psychic development, protection, prophetic dreams, legal matters, psychic powers, healing (may cause drowsiness, avoid if on sedatives)

CAYENNE PEPPER Fidelity, hex breaking, protection, removal of blocks and negative energy, overcoming obstacles, fire, strength, passion (avoid taking with medications that slow blood-clotting and with theophylline)

CHAMOMILE Protection, luck, money, sleep, peace, purification (may decrease effectiveness of birth-control pills and some cancer medications, and may increase the effects of warfarin; discuss usage with your doctor if you are taking medication for your liver)

CINNAMON Sexuality, lust, wealth, money, consecration, purification, love (avoid taking with diabetes medications)

DANDELION (both root and leaf) Purification, manifestation of wishes, enrichment, money (avoid if on antibiotics, lithium, or water pills; discuss usage with your doctor if you are taking medication for your liver)

ELDERBERRY Exorcism, protection, healing, prosperity, sleep, protection against witchcraft (avoid taking with medications that decrease the immune system)

GINGER Love, money, success, power, protection (avoid taking with medications that slow blood-clotting)

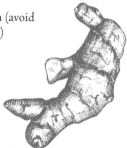

GINKGO Healing, mental clarity, fertility; avoid taking with ibuprofen or with medications that slow blood-clotting; numerous medications have interactions with ginkgo, discuss usage with your health-care practitioner before taking)

GINSENG Fertility, sexuality, lust, manifestation of wishes, healing, beauty, protection (do *not* take with medications that slow blood-clotting; avoid taking with diabetes medications or with MAO inhibitors)

GOLDENROD Money, divination (may cause drowsiness, avoid taking with sedatives)

LAVENDER Love, protection, purification, happiness, peace, healing, meditation, psychic abilities (may cause drowsiness, avoid taking with sedatives)

LEMON BALM Love, success, healing, cleansing (may cause drowsiness, avoid taking with sedatives)

NETTLE LEAF Protection, exorcism, healing, jinx-breaking, lust (avoid taking with sedatives, lithium, or medications for diabetes, for high blood pressure, or that slow blood-clotting)

PARSLEY Healing, fortune, success, lust, protection, purification, ancestor veneration, working with the dead, traveling to the land of the dead, calling upon the energy of death and decay (do *not* take with medications that slow blood-clotting or with diuretics)

PEPPERMINT Purification, love, healing, psychic powers (avoid if you have acid-reflux disease; avoid taking with cyclosporine; discuss usage with your doctor if you are taking any medications that are changed by the liver)

PINE NEEDLES Removal of evil, money, cleansing, healing, fertility, protection, exorcism

ROSEMARY Cleansing, drawing the aid of spirits, love, mental focus, protection, lust, exorcism, healing

THYME Health, healing, sleep, psychic powers, love, purification, courage, good luck (do *not* take with medications that slow blood-clotting)

Working with Spirits

One can connect with spirits through meditation, prayer, and trance work. There are many different ways to work with spirits—from prayers and maintaining shrines to calling on them in spells and rituals. Some herbs, such as parsley, can assist you in this endeavor. When you work with a spirit, you contact them and ask them to assist you with your spells or rituals.

To make a magickal tea, look at the properties of the herbs and choose the ones you feel would best suit the work ahead. Don't be afraid to tap into the different associations of the herbs for specific work. For instance, calendula is good for protection, money, and prosperity. You could use this tea to know that your money or financial stability is protected and that you will continue to be prosperous and successful. By adding pine to the tea, you would have the powers of fertility and money to draw on, adding an element of fertility that will keep your money flowing.

Magickal Tea Recipes

The following teas are designed for specific magickal purposes. The money teas attract money and protect it, which will reduce stress around detrimental financial situations. The spirit-aid tea is there to help you meet your spirit guides and helpers. The protection teas enhance your spiritual protection while removing any negative energies. The cleansing tea removes negativity and brings blessings. The psychic-enhancement tea opens psychic channels, and the divination tea allows for clarity during divination.

Important note: The amounts listed here are for dried herbs, flowers, and spices. Dried ingredients are preferred for teas. If you wish to use fresh ingredients for decoctions, and they are available, double the amount. See cautions and interactions in the herb list on pages 205–207.

Attract and Protect Money

- ¼ teaspoon goldenrod
- ¼ teaspoon chamomile
- ¼ teaspoon basil

Spirit Aid

- ¼ teaspoon parsley
- ¼ teaspoon rosemary

Love and Lust

- ⅛ teaspoon cinnamon
- ¼ teaspoon catnip
- ¼ teaspoon ginseng

Exorcism

- ¼ teaspoon angelica root
- ¼ teaspoon nettle leaf
- ¼ teaspoon elder flower

Cleansing

- ¼ teaspoon dandelion
- ¼ teaspoon lemon balm
- ¼ teaspoon thyme

Protection

- ¼ teaspoon pine needles
- ¼ teaspoon elderberries
- ¼ teaspoon blackberry leaf

Divination

- ¼ teaspoon goldenrod
- ¼ teaspoon peppermint

Psychic Development

- ¼ teaspoon calendula (marigold)
- ¼ teaspoon ginkgo leaf
- ¼ teaspoon lavender

TINCTURES AND TONICS FOR HEALTH

Tinctures and tonics are two fun and easy home remedies. A tincture is traditionally an herbal infusion made with an alcohol base. A tonic, on the other hand, always uses either vegetable glycerin or apple cider vinegar as the base. The alcohol used in tinctures must be at least 100 proof, or 50 percent, alcohol, which is why most vodkas and gins can be used to create tinctures. For people who have difficulties dealing with alcohol of any type, tinctures can also be made with vegetable glycerin or apple cider vinegar. Tinctures made with these other two options will not be as potent, but they will still be effective as home remedies.

Crafting Tinctures and Tonics

The tools needed for crafting tinctures and tonics are fairly simple. You need two mason jars; cheesecloth; the herbs, plants, or spices you are using; measuring cups; an herb grinder; and alcohol for tinctures, or vegetable glycerin or apple cider vinegar for tonics. Once the remedies are prepared, you will need a tool to measure dosage. The droppers sold at your local pharmacy for infant medication will work well for this.

The general steps for creating all the recipes in this section are the same. You prepare the ingredients and then fill the mason jar with the herbs, plants, or spices. Add the alcohol or alcohol substitute. (If you are using apple cider vinegar as your base, you will need to take the additional step of laying wax paper on top of the jar and draping it over the jar mouth threads before screwing on the jar lid). Keep in a cool, dark place for a month (some may require refrigeration, and that will be noted), and shake twice daily. After a month, strain the herbal matter from the liquid into the second jar using a cheesecloth (squeeze the cheesecloth to get out as much of the liquid as you can). After straining, fill the remainder of the jar with distilled water. This dilutes the alcohol, allowing you to ingest it directly. You now have a prepared remedy.

When preparing a tincture, the rule of thumb is that you want a 1:4 ratio of herb to alcohol. For each part (total) herb, you want four parts alcohol. One way to gauge your ratio is to cover the herbs with the alcohol until the herbs start to float. Allow the herbs to start absorbing the alcohol and settle down a bit, then add a little more alcohol until the mixture is fully saturated.

Herbs and Plants for Health Tinctures and Tonics

The following herbs and plants are best used in tinctures or tonics. Some herbs work best when they are combined with other herbs in the tincture or tonic. Many of these blends may not taste all that good, but they will work.

ALFALFA Energy booster, laxative, cleanser (avoid taking with medications that slow blood-clotting or suppress the immune system and with birth-control pills)

ALLSPICE Stimulant; eases indigestion, colds, coughs; reduces hives and swelling (avoid taking with medications that slow blood-clotting)

ALOE VERA JUICE (liquid) Soothes the skin, antiseptic (external use only)

ANGELICA (fruit or seeds) Eases indigestion, gas, gout; balances nervous system (do *not* use if you are diabetic)

BAY LEAF Eases indigestion, coughs, colds, fevers (do *not* take with any narcotics or sedatives)

BEARBERRY (*Arctostaphylos uva-ursi*) Antiseptic, eases symptoms of urinary tract infections (do *not* use if you are pregnant or breastfeeding or if you have stomach irritation or kidney disease; avoid taking with lithium)

BERGAMOT Soothes colds, fevers, coughs, nausea, indigestion, menstrual cramps (avoid taking with photosensitizing medications)

BLACK-EYED SUSAN Soothes swelling, back pain, earaches; immune booster

BLACK PEPPERCORN Anti-fungal, heals ulcers, relieves arthritis

BURDOCK ROOT Detoxifying, soothes colds and skin issues
(avoid taking with medications that slow blood-clotting)

CEDAR (freshly dried leafy twigs) Soothes gout, naturally antiviral,
boosts immune system (may cause drowsiness, avoid if on sedatives)

CLOVER (red) Soothes coughs, colds, bronchitis (avoid taking with
medications that slow blood-clotting and with tamoxifen; may decrease
effectiveness of birth-control pills and medications that are changed
by the liver)

CLOVES Soothes nausea and indigestion; antiseptic, expectorant
(avoid taking with medications that slow blood-clotting)

COMFREY LEAF Eases arthritis, rheumatism, coughs, colds, diarrhea,
asthma; antibacterial (do *not* take with medications that can harm the liver)

CORIANDER SEEDS Aids in digestion; aphrodisiac; boots immune system

CRAMP BARK Eases arthritis, rheumatism, menstrual cramps

ECHINACEA Eases colds, antibacterial, anti-inflammatory, boosts
immune system (interacts with various medications, discuss usage
with your health-care practitioner before taking)

GARLIC Antiseptic; eases atherosclerosis, rheumatism,
ear infections, symptoms of urinary tract infections;
supports healthy cholesterol; helps lower blood
pressure; boosts immune system; expectorant;
reduces risks of colon, rectal, and prostate
cancers (do *not* take with isoniazid, medications
used for HIV/AIDS, or medications used to
slow blood-clotting)

GOLDENSEAL (roots and leaves) Aids digestion; eases colds, hay fever, menstrual cramps (avoid taking with medications that are changed by the liver)

HORSERADISH Antiseptic; antibacterial; expectorant; soothes flu, colds, coughs, symptoms of urinary tract infections; diuretic; appetite stimulant; (avoid taking with thyroid medications)

HYSSOP Soothes colds, fevers, sore throats, asthma, rheumatism, indigestion; expectorant

LEMON Boosts immune system, helps prevent kidney stones, eases indigestion and constipation, relieves toothaches

LEMONGRASS Supports healthy cholesterol; antibacterial; detoxifies; relieves constipation, nausea, diarrhea, insomnia, coughs, colds, fevers, anxiety, stress, fatigue; boosts immune system

MUGWORT Eases menstrual cramps, stomach cramps, fevers, colds (do *not* take if pregnant)

MULLEIN Relieves asthma, coughs, colds, diarrhea, hemorrhoids; expectorant; diuretic

NUTMEG Stimulates digestive system; relieves diarrhea, nausea, anxiety (avoid taking with medications that are changed by the liver)

ORANGE Lowers blood pressure, reduces cholesterol, relieves arthritis and anxiety, stabilizes mood, boosts immune system; laxative (do *not* take with celiprolol, ivermectin, or pravastatin)

ONION Helps lower systolic blood pressure, eases colds; antiseptic (avoid taking with medications that slow blood-clotting)

SKULLCAP Eases headaches, stress, menstrual tension, insomnia, anxiety; sedative

TURMERIC Anti-inflammatory, reduces cholesterol (avoid taking with medications that slow blood-clotting)

VALERIAN ROOT Eases insomnia (do *not* take with alcohol, sedatives, or antianxiety medications

WITCH HAZEL BARK Relieves pain, diarrhea, colds, fevers, ulcers, colitis; antiseptic

WORMWOOD Eases indigestion and stomach disorders; aphrodisiac (avoid taking with anticonvulsant medications)

YARROW Antiseptic, relieves pain, hay fever, colds, fevers, menstrual cramps (do *not* take with medications that slow blood-clotting, avoid taking with lithium or sedatives)

YELLOW DOCK Laxative; reduces anemia, relieves fatigue, aids digestive system (do *not* take with digoxin, diuretic medications, or medications that slow blood-clotting)

TINCTURE RECIPES FOR COMMON HEALTH ISSUES

It's time to start making tinctures. Once a tincture is made, it has an approximate one-year shelf life. The dosage for a tincture is one to three drops directly under your tongue, two to three times a day as needed, for up to seven to ten days. You can add the tinctures to a small amount of water or juice if you have a hard time taking a direct dose.

See cautions and interactions in the herb list on pages 212–123. *Note: For all of these recipes, the herbs and spices can be either dried and ground, or dried and finely chopped, unless otherwise specified.*

Arthritis and Gout

Arthritis Relief

Note: This tincture can be used externally as well as internally as needed.

- ¼ cup (60 ml) aloe vera juice (liquid)
- 4 tablespoons black peppercorn
- ½ cup (26 g) cramp bark, ground
- ½ cup (56 g) turmeric, ground
- 6 cups (1.4 L) alcohol

Gout Relief

Note: External use only.

- ½ cup (16 g) angelica leaf
- ½ cup (50 g) bearberry (*Arctostaphylos uva-ursi*)
- 4 tablespoons black-eyed Susan
- ¼ cup (26 g) cedar, leafy twigs, broken up and finely chopped
- 6 cups (1.4 L) alcohol

"Anti" Remedies

Note: All "Anti" tinctures in this section are for external use only.
To use, apply a few drops to the affected area.

Antibacterial

4 tablespoons comfrey leaf
½ cup (16 g) echinacea flowers
4 tablespoons lemongrass stalks, finely chopped
1 tablespoon turmeric, ground
4 cups (960 ml) alcohol

Antifungal

4 tablespoons black peppercorn
½ cup (56 g) turmeric, ground
4 cups (960 ml) alcohol

Antimicrobial

¼ cup (60 ml) aloe vera juice (liquid)
½ cup (16 g) echinacea flowers
2 garlic cloves, chopped
½ cup (40 g) goldenseal root
¼ cup (3.5 g) horseradish
8 cups (1.9 L) alcohol

Antiseptic

¼ cup (25 g) bearberry (*Arctostaphylos uva-ursi*)
4 tablespoons cloves
½ cup (16 g) yarrow leaves
½ cup (26 g) witch hazel bark
6 cups (1.4 L) alcohol

Anxiety and Stress

Anxiety Relief

½ cup (40 g) valerian root, ground
1 cup (225 g) orange peel, dried and chopped
½ cup (16 g) skullcap leaves
6 cups (1.4 L) alcohol

Stress Relief

4 tablespoons lemongrass stalks, finely chopped
4 tablespoons skullcap
4 cups (950 ml) alcohol

Blood Pressure, Blood Sugar, and Cholesterol

Helps Reduce Blood Pressure

- 4 cloves garlic, chopped
- 1/2 cup (75 g) onion, chopped
- 4 cups (960 ml) alcohol

Blood Sugar Balancing

- 4 tablespoons alfalfa
- 1/4 cup (56 g) lemon peel, chopped
- 4 cups (960 ml) alcohol

Helps Reduce Cholesterol

- 2 cloves garlic, chopped
- 1/2 cup (32 g) lemongrass stalks, finely chopped
- 1/2 cup (112 g) orange peel, dried and chopped
- 6 cups (1.4 L) alcohol

Colds, Coughs, and Respiratory Issues

Cold Relief

- 1 tablespoon ground allspice
- 5 bay leaves
- 1/2 cup (75 g) onion
- 1/2 cup (16 g) clover leaves, fresh
- 1 cup (225 g) orange peel, dried and chopped
- 8 cups (1.9 L) alcohol

Expectorant

- 4 tablespoons cloves
- 1/4 cup (16 g) hyssop flowers
- 4 cups (1.4 L) alcohol

Soothe Breathing

- 1/4 cup (16 g) comfrey leaf
- 1/2 cup (16 g) hyssop
- 1/4 cup (56 g) lemon peel, dried and chopped
- 1/2 cup (16 g) mullein leaves
- 6 cups (1.4 L) alcohol

Fevers and Flu

Fever Break

- 2 tablespoons cayenne pepper
- 5 bay leaves
- 1 cup (14 g) horseradish
- ½ cup (16 g) mugwort
- 6 cups (1.4 L) alcohol

Flu Relief

- 5 bay leaves
- 1 cup (32 g) hyssop
- 1 tablespoon ground turmeric
- 6 cups (1.4 L) alcohol

Constipation, Diarrhea, Indigestion, and Nausea Relief

Nausea Relief

- ½ cup (52 g) cloves
- ½ (43 g) cup ginger
- ¼ cup (16 g) lemongrass stalks, finely chopped
- 6 cups (1.4 L) alcohol

Diarrhea Relief

- ½ cup (120 ml) aloe vera juice (liquid)
- ½ cup (16 g) comfrey leaf
- ¼ cup (16 g) lemongrass stalks, finely chopped
- 4 tablespoons mullein
- 6 cups (1.4 L) alcohol

Indigestion Relief

- 1 tablespoon bergamot leaves
- ½ cup (16 g) hyssop
- 4 tablespoons wormwood
- 8 cups (1.9 L) alcohol

Digestion Boost

- 1 tablespoon nutmeg
- ½ cup (40 g) coriander seeds
- 4 tablespoons goldenseal
- ½ cup (16 g) lemon balm
- ½ cup (16 g) yellow dock
- 8 cups (1.9 L) alcohol

Constipation Relief

- ½ cup (16 g) alfalfa
- ½ cup (112 g) lemon peel, dried and chopped
- ½ cup (49 g) goldenseal root
- ½ cup (16 g) yellow dock
- 8 cups (1.9 L) alcohol

Aids for Fatigue, Sleep, and Mood Stabilization

Fatigue Relief

- 1 tablespoon allspice
- 4 tablespoons alfalfa
- ½ cup (32 g) lemongrass stalks, finely chopped
- ½ cup (16 g) yellow dock
- 8 cups (1.9 L) alcohol

Sleep Aid

- 1 cup chamomile
- ½ cup (16 g) lavender
- ½ cup (32 g) lemongrass stalks, finely chopped
- 1 cup peppermint
- ½ cup (16 g) skullcap
- ½ cup (40 g) valerian root
- 12 cups (2.8 L) alcohol

Mood Stabilizer

- ½ cup (16 g) angelica leaf
- ½ cup (112 g) dried orange peel, chopped
- 4 cups (960 ml) alcohol

Immune Boosters

Immune Booster

- ½ cup (16 g) black-eyed Susan
- ½ cup (16 g) echinacea
- 4 tablespoons coriander seeds
- ½ cup (112 g) orange peel, dried and chopped
- 8 cups (1.9 L) alcohol

Antiviral

- 10–15 cedar bark chips
- ¼ cup (56 g) lemon peel, dried and chopped
- ¼ cup (56 g) orange peel, dried and chopped
- ½ cup (7 g) horseradish
- 1 tablespoon ground turmeric
- 6 cups (1.4 L) alcohol

Additional Remedies

Menstrual Cramps Relief

½ cup (26 g) cramp bark, dried and
　　ground
½ cup (16 g) mugwort
4 tablespoons skullcap
4 tablespoons yarrow
6 cups (1.4 L) alcohol

Urinary Tract Infection Symptom Relief

¼ cup (50 g) bearberry
　　(*Arctostaphylos uva-ursi*)
4 tablespoons black-eyed Susan
4 garlic cloves, chopped
½ cup (7 g) horseradish
4 tablespoons yarrow
8 cups (1.9 L) alcohol

Ulcer Relief

1 tablespoon black peppercorn
1 tablespoon ground turmeric
½ cup (120 ml) aloe vera juice (liquid)
½ cup (26 g) witch hazel bark
4 cups (960 ml) alcohol

Ear Infections

1 cup (32 g) black-eyed Susan
2 garlic cloves, chopped
4 tablespoons basil
8 cups (1.9 L) alcohol

Hemorrhoids

Note: External use only.
½ cup (16 g) mullein
½ cup (16 g) yarrow
4 cups (960 ml) alcohol

MAGICKAL TINCTURES

Tinctures are an excellent way to work with your spiritual power. They can be burned as incense, used to anoint candles, worn as a perfume, or ingested—depending on the work at hand. Alcohol is a common offering to spirits. When working with tinctures, the alcohol base activates the spirits in the plants. It feeds the spirit, allowing the energy of the spirit to be infused into the tincture. Magickal workings with tinctures tap into the deep powers within our own spirits as well as the spirits of the plant.

When making a tincture for use in magick and spirituality, the tincture is charged with prayers and blessings. Shake the tincture two times a day to direct your energy into the jar and activate the magick within the herbs. Say a prayer or blessing as you shake—you can use the one on page 195 if you wish.

Tincture-Charging Spell

Use this process to empower the tinctures while you create them.

Materials

- 1 green candle (herb spirits)
- 1 white candle (spirit and magick)
- 1 candle to charge the tincture (color depends on spell: gold for money, red for love, blue for healing, etc.)
- 1 mixing bowl

  Herbs and alcohol for the tincture (see recipes on pages 216–221)
- 2 mason jars

  Cheesecloth

Ritual

Place the three candles in a triangle on your altar or workspace. The white candle should be the top of the triangle (facing away from you to direct the energy out into the universe); the green and other color candle form the base.

Place the bowl at the center of the altar, and place your containers of herbs and alcohol on the floor.

Light the white candle while stating:

"For the power of spirit."

Light the green candle while stating:

"For the herbal spirits."

Light the colored candle for your need, and state your need.

Place an herb in the bowl, state a thank-you blessing to the herb, and explain why you are using that herb. Repeat for each herb, and as you add each herb, stir the mixture of herbs clockwise for increasing or bringing something to you and counterclockwise if you are trying to remove or decrease something in your life (banishments, reversals, removals, etc.).

Once you have mixed all of the herbs in the bowl, hold your hands over the mixture and state your intent. Visualize a light coming out of your hands for that need (red for love and passion or power; green for money, success, growth and fertility; blue for healing; yellow for success; and so on).

Pour the mixture into one of the mason jars and add the alcohol (do this at a safe distance from the lit candles). Place the lid on the jar.

Remove the mixing bowl from the altar and put the mason jar with the tincture blend in its place, in the center of the candles. Keep the mason jar there until the candles have finished burning.

Shake the tincture, focusing your mental, emotional, and physical energy into the jar. As you shake the jar, chant:

> *"I call upon the powers green,*
> *Release the powers unseen.*
> *Herbs awakened on this day,*
> *Blessings in this tincture stay."*

Shake the jar twice daily for one month, each time visualizing the need behind the tincture.

Once the month has passed, strain the mixture into the second jar using cheesecloth. Now the tincture is ready to be used in magickal work.

HERBS FOR MAGICKAL TINCTURES

All of the herbs used in the health tinctures on pages 216–221 also have magickal and spiritual attributes—these attributes are listed here. For magickal uses, the following herbs, spices, and plants are only for external use in tincture blends.

ANGELICA LEAF Angel work, protection, removing hexes, exorcism, health, meditation, divination

ALFALFA Money attraction (drawing money to you), prosperity, protection

ALLSPICE Money, luck, healing

ALOE VERA Protection, peace in the afterlife, prosperity, success, love

BAY LEAF Protection, purification, enhancing psychic powers, strength

BEARBERRY (*Arctostaphylos uva-ursi*) Victory, protection, money, power, strength

BERGAMOT Money, clarity

BLACK-EYED SUSAN Cleansing, releasing, grounding, integration, mediumship, connecting with the dead

BLACK PEPPERCORN Protection, exorcism

BURDOCK ROOT Protection, uncrossing (removing hexes or curses)

CEDAR Healing, purification, money, protection

CLOVER Protection, money, fidelity, love, exorcism, success

CLOVES Enhancing psychic powers, astral travel, protection, exorcism, love

COMFREY LEAF Money, safe travel, protection

CORIANDER SEEDS Love, health, healing, lust, fidelity

CRAMP BARK Protection, luck

ECHINACEA Strengthening spells, offerings to spirits

GARLIC Protection, exorcism, lust, antitheft

GOLDENSEAL Healing, money

HORSERADISH Purification, exorcism

HYSSOP Purification, protection, cleansing

LEMON Purification, love, friendship, justice

LEMONGRASS Repelling snakes, lust, enhancing psychic powers

MUGWORT Strength, psychic powers, protection, prophetic dreams, astral projection

MULLEIN Courage, protection, love, divination, exorcism

NUTMEG Gambling luck, money, fidelity, prosperity, luck

ORANGE Love, divination, luck, money

ONION Protection, exorcism, money, prophetic dreams, lust

SAINT JOHN'S WORT Health, protection, strength, love, divination, happiness

SKULLCAP Love, fidelity, peace

TURMERIC Purification

VALERIAN ROOT Purification, cleansing, peace, love, protection, breaking hexes and curses

WORMWOOD Summoning spirits, working with the dead, enhancing psychic power, protection, love, prophesizing, breaking hexes and curses

WITCH HAZEL Protection, chasteness (less likely to give into temptation and sexual desire)

YARROW Psychic development, courage, love, exorcism, protection

YELLOW DOCK Money attraction, customer attraction, love attraction

MAGICKAL TINCTURE BLENDS

The following blends are for magickal and spiritual use only. They can be used in spells, rituals, and meditations. They can be worn as perfumes, poured into baths, or used to anoint candles. As noted previously, they are for *external use only*. These tincture blends carry the spiritual essence of the herbs, so they are very potent forces for magickal and spiritual work.

Note: With all of these recipes, the herbs and spices can be either dried and ground, or dried and chopped finely, unless otherwise specified.

Business Success and Luck

Lucky Business

- ½ cup (16 g) alfalfa
- 2 tablespoons allspice
- 1 cup (80 g) goldenseal root
- 8 cups (1.9 L) alcohol

Increase Luck

- 2 tablespoons allspice
- 1 tablespoon bergamot leaves, dried
- 2 tablespoons nutmeg
- ½ cup (26 g) cramp bark, dried and ground
- 4 cups (960 ml) alcohol

Love and Lust

Sweetly Love Me

- 1 tablespoon cloves
- ½ cup (120 ml) aloe vera juice (liquid)
- ½ cup (112 g) lemon peel, dried and chopped
- ½ cup (112 g) orange peel, dried and chopped
- ½ cup (16 g) yellow dock
- 8 cups (1.9 L) alcohol

Lovely Lust
(Ensures Lust and Love are Paired Together)

- ½ cup (40 g) coriander seeds
- ½ cup (32 g) lemongrass stalks, finely chopped
- 4 tablespoons skullcap
- 4 tablespoons Saint John's wort
- 6 cups (1.4 L) alcohol

Hex-Breaking, Protection, and Cleansing

Hex Breaker

- 4 tablespoons angelica root, dried and ground
- 4 tablespoons burdock root, dried and ground
- ½ cup (40 g) valerian root, dried and ground
- ½ cup (16 g) wormwood leaves flower tops, dried and ground
- 6 cups (1.4 L) alcohol

Hex Banisher
(Cleanses, Removes, Reverses, Protects)

- 5 bay leaves
- ½ cup (16 g) black-eyed Susan
- 3–5 cedar chips
- 8 cups (1.9 L) alcohol

Protect From and Remove Evil

- ¼ cup (25 g) bearberry (*Arctostaphylos uva-ursi*)
- 4 tablespoons black peppercorn
- ½ cup (16 g) clover
- 4 tablespoons horseradish
- ½ cup (16 g) mullein
- 8 cups (1.9 L) alcohol

Cleanse and Purify

- ½ cup (112 g) lemon peel, dried and chopped
- ½ cup (16 g) hyssop
- 1 tablespoon ground turmeric
- 4 cups (960 ml) alcohol

Astral Travel and Enhancing Psychic Abilities

Astral Travel

- ½ cup (52 g) cloves
- ½ cup (16 g) mugwort
- 4 cups (960 ml) alcohol

Psychic Development

- ½ cup (16 g) mugwort
- ½ cup (16 g) wormwood
- 4 tablespoons yarrow
- 6 cups (1.4 L) alcohol

Spirit Offering (Burned as an Offering)

- ½ cup (16 g) black-eyed Susan
- ½ cup (16 g) echinacea
- ½ cup (16 g) wormwood
- 6 cups (1.4 L) alcohol

HOLISTIC WATERS
AND VINEGAR TONICS

Healing the body, mind, and spirit using holistic herbal remedies is a tradition found across the world in cultures where the health of the spirit and the body are believed to be integrally connected. The remedies were often—and still are—crafted and created to address both the magickal (or spiritual) aspects and the physical aspects of ailments.

Frankincense Water

One of the most commonly burned spiritual resins is frankincense, the hardened gumlike substance tapped from Boswellia trees. This resin is believed to have many medicinal qualities, including being antifungal, anti-inflammatory, a digestive aid, a diuretic, an expectorant, and having antioxidant properties. It has been shown to help symptoms of arthritis and is in the early phases of being tested for cancer prevention.

In ancient times, frankincense was revered as a holy resin for incense and healing remedies, and it is believed that ancient healers were well aware of its anti-inflammatory properties. It is well-known as one of the gifts presented by the Magi to baby Jesus in the manger. Spiritually, its attributes include purification, blessing, protection, exorcism, and spirituality.

This remedy comes from the Middle East, where frankincense resin is naturally found. Remedies such as this have been used in the region, as well as in India, for millennia.

(Note: This water can also be used to protect yourself in a health or healing spell. Medicinal properties will combine with the spiritual properties of the resin to destroy any harmful spirit essence.)

Ingredients

- 4–5 medium chunks of frankincense resin (make sure the resin you buy is safe for placing in water that you are going to drink), rinsed free of dust and dirt

- 4 cups (960 ml) purified, distilled water (do *not* use tap water)

Place the resin in the bottom of a 1-quart (960-ml) glass jar.

Boil the water and pour it over the resin. Cover with a plate or towel and set in a cool, dry, dark place. Let sit overnight.

Dosage: Drink a few ounces throughout the day. If you are new to this remedy, drink it slowly to see how your body responds. You can even dilute it by mixing a ½ cup (120 ml) of the resin water with plain tap water while you adjust to the flavor and properties.

Four Thieves Vinegar

Four Thieves Vinegar is noted to have a few different health benefits, from boosting the immune system to speeding up recovery from a cold or the flu. When you look at the ingredients it contains, you can see that it is a truly holistic remedy: it treats spiritual issues (cleansing and removing spiritual toxins) as well as physical issues (the garlic, herbs, and spices have multiple healing and detoxifying properties).

American herbalist Rosemary Gladstar mentions in her book *Rosemary Gladstar's Medicinal Herbs* that this vinegar was historically used by gypsies and witches to protect against spells and witchcraft, as well as to protect their homes against thieves. Other traditions, such as hoodoo and ceremonial magick, have employed this tonic for removing and banishing negative forces and for spiritual cleansing.

Ingredients

- 5 cloves garlic, chopped or minced
- ½ cup rosemary, fresh and chopped
- 4 tablespoons lavender, dried
- 2 tablespoons hyssop
- 1 tablespoon cayenne pepper
- 1 tablespoon black peppercorn
- 4 cups (960 ml) apple cider vinegar

Place the garlic, herbs, and spices in a glass jar 1 quart (960 ml) in size or larger.

Slightly warm the apple cider vinegar and pour over the mixture in the jar. Stir or shake well and let sit for four to six weeks in a cool, dark place. When ready, strain the vinegar through cheesecloth into a new bottle.

Dosage: For prevention, take 1 tablespoon daily as needed during cold and flu season. When sick, take 1 tablespoon two to three times daily to speed up recovery.

Fire Cider

This tonic is related to Four Thieves Vinegar, as they share some ingredients and have similar uses. Fire Cider may have developed as an alternative to Four Thieves, which had an association with outcasts, witches, and thieves.

Fire Cider is a potent tonic. It has several ingredients, including horseradish, that fight the fevers that often occur with flus, making this a powerhouse of a tonic. Medicinally, this tonic can be used as an antiseptic, an antibacterial, an antibiotic, a diuretic, an expectorant, and to treat the flu, colds, whooping cough, and urinary tract infections. It is also an appetite stimulant. This brew will help you be happy and healthy. It will boost your immune system and remove any and all toxins from your system.

Spiritually, you can use Fire Cider to cleanse your body of negativity and protect it from new negative influences. It also works to remove and reverse anything that has been sent your way. This will allow you to invite luck, love, and money all at once. This truly is an all-purpose tonic that cleanses and removes blocks so love, luck, money, and success can bloom.

Ingredients

- ½ cup (7 g) horseradish
- 1 garlic clove
- 1 onion
- 1 lemon, peeled and quartered
- 1 orange, peeled and quartered
- ¼ tablespoon cayenne pepper
- ¼ teaspoon turmeric, ground
- 1 tablespoon black peppercorn
- 1 teaspoon ginger, fresh
- 3 teaspoons (or about 5 fresh sprigs) rosemary, dried
- 1 habanero pepper, finely chopped
- 1–2 quarts (1–2 L) apple cider vinegar
- Honey to taste

Finely chop the horseradish, garlic, onion, lemon, and orange, and place them in a large glass jar, 1 quart (960 ml) in size or larger. Mix in the cayenne pepper, turmeric, black peppercorn, ginger, rosemary, and habanero. Cover with the apple cider vinegar. Take a piece of parchment paper, lay it over the mouth of the jar, firmly secure the lid, and shake.

Store in the fridge for four weeks, shaking once daily. When ready, strain through cheesecloth into a fresh jar, and add honey to taste.

Dosage: For prevention, take 1 tablespoon daily as needed to boost the immune system. When sick, take 2 tablespoons, three times daily as needed.

Carmelite Water

It is believed that the Carmelite order of monks or nuns created this water sometime in the seventeenth century, when it was primarily used as a cologne of sorts. It is not as well-known as Four Thieves Vinegar, but it is a widely used water that is great for helping with digestion and anxiety.

The connection between the mind, body, and spirit is amazing. Often anxiety and health issues are tied together. When we are anxious, we can suffer from indigestion, as well as insomnia and, occasionally, depression. This tonic addresses several of those ailments at once.

Spiritually, this tonic is used as a road opener (removing blocks), cleanser (banishing and removing energy), and for blessings. In magick and spiritual work, you can use the tonic to remove and protect against negativity (reversal of energy and protection from its return). This opens the path to success, allowing for love and luck to bloom.

Ingredients

- 1 cup (32 g) lemon balm
- ½ cup (16 g) angelica leaves and stems, chopped
- 1 tablespoon cloves
- 1 lemon, zested

- ½ tablespoon nutmeg
- 1 teaspoon coriander seeds, bruised
- 4 cups (960 ml) vodka, gin, or brandy

Place the dry ingredients in a 1-quart (960 ml) glass jar, and add the alcohol. Stir and shake well. Place in a cool, dry place and let steep for two weeks. Strain through cheesecloth into a new jar. It will keep for up to six months.

Dosage: One tablespoon daily as needed to aid in digestion or to soothe anxiety.

HONEY-SYRUP RECIPES

Whenever we get a cold or flu, one of the most common things we do is run to the store and pick up a bottle of cough syrup. The use of syrups to fight coughs, colds, and flu is not a new thing. Our ancestors used a variety of different syrups to treat these common ailments. Today, many of these syrups are becoming popular again as home remedies. The primary ingredient is honey, which has a natural antiseptic property that kills off bacteria. Plus, it tastes good, which makes taking the medicine easy.

Garlic Honey for Sore Throats and Coughs

Both garlic and honey have natural antiseptic properties that help remove bacteria-causing illnesses. This remedy does not spoil, so one batch will last up to a year.

Ingredients

- 1 garlic bulb, separated into cloves and peeled
- 2–4 ounces (59–118 ml) honey

Place the garlic cloves in a 4- to 8-ounce (118- to 236-ml) jar. Pour the honey over the garlic cloves so they are completely covered and the container is filled about halfway. Using chopsticks or a fork, poke the honey into the garlic. Let steep for twenty-four hours.

Dosage: Take by the spoonful as needed, or simply eat the garlic-infused honey with food.

Onion-and-Garlic Honey for Coughs, Colds, and Flu

This honey is similar to Garlic Honey, except onions are added to the mix. Garlic and onions have similar antiseptic properties, and they are also used in similar applications for cold and flu relief.

Ingredients

- 4 garlic cloves, chopped
- 1 small onion, chopped
- 1 cup elderberries
- Honey, enough to cover the garlic, onion, and berries and fill the container about halfway
- 1 teaspoon cloves
- 1 teaspoon cinnamon

Place the garlic, onion, and elderberries at the bottom of a 1-quart (960 ml) glass mason jar. Cover them with honey and then mix in the cloves and cinnamon. Stir well and let steep for forty-eight hours before using.

Dosage: 1 tablespoon as needed.

Elderberry Syrup

Elderberry Syrup is a very common folk remedy. If you feel a bug coming on, take it daily to help prevent you from getting a cough, cold, or flu. If you take Elderberry Syrup while already ill, it may reduce the amount of time that you are sick.

Ingredients

- 2 cups blue elderberries
- 1 teaspoon cinnamon
- 1 teaspoon cloves
- 1 teaspoon ginger
- 5 cups (1.2 L) water
- Honey (see instructions for quantity)

Place the ingredients except for the honey in a medium saucepan and bring to a boil. Once boiling, reduce the heat to a simmer (low-medium heat) for thirty minutes. Strain the mixture through a cheesecloth into a 1-quart (960 ml) glass mason jar. Mash the berries and herbs together to express all the remaining juice. Measure the amount of liquid and add the same amount of honey. Stir and mix well. It is ready to use once cooled to room temperature.

Store in a cool and dry place for up to twelve weeks.

Dosage: For prevention, take 1 tablespoon daily to boost the immune system. When sick, take 2 tablespoons every two to three hours daily as needed.

> "May the wisdom of the green world provide
> You with health, wealth, and prosperity.
> So mote it be."

Chapter 8

Kitchen Witchyware

COOKING UP
MAGICK

Most witches today favor a particular practice within the craft—kitchen or hearth witches work with herbal remedies, potions, and crystals. When it comes to knowing what to eat, this is where the crafty kitchen witch excels. Traditional witch types study and worship the ancient ways. Green witches practice earth-based folk law. Hedge witches like to be outdoors and one with nature, scouring the hedgerows for berries and herbs. Hedge witches also use a lot of natural elements, such as crystals and stones, in their craft and will work their magick by the phases of the moon and the natural environment. Kitchen witchery is very similar. These witches enjoy gathering their craft items from the great outdoors, but they are a little more hands-on in the kitchen and may even grow their own produce in a kitchen garden. They cook up magickal foods from their yields and make natural herbal potions using the plants they have gathered over time. Many kitchen witches make it their mission to learn about the properties of herbs and plants. It is not unusual to see plants they will use in medicinal teas and recipes hanging to dry in their windows. They focus a great deal on curing ailments, but they also bless and charge the plants to make magickal pouches that can be carried to cure other everyday problems.

Witches in the twenty-first century also have a deep understanding and respect for everything living in our natural world, and they are thankful for all of the earth's offerings. They believe in the energies of the universe and are emphatic about keeping everything as calm and balanced as possible. For us to live and love in a harmonious way, it is imperative that we all strive for the same equilibrium.

In this chapter, we'll explore different types of witchery, especially as they relate to Sabbats, or Wiccan Sabbaths. There are a lot of delicious recipes to try in this chapter—all from the recipe collections of real witches!

YOU ARE WHAT YOU EAT!

Within the Wiccan community, there is a strong belief that just as every living thing on the planet holds energy, so does the food we eat—and what we eat, we become. If we consume an animal that was unhappy in its life, we are in turn absorbing that stressful and unhappy energy, allowing it to circulate through our bodies. If the chef cooking the food had a meltdown or spent his cooking time screeching profanities at his assistant, the plate of food in front of you has been spiritually contaminated. On the other hand, a yummy slice of homemade carrot cake that was baked by someone who loves you will make you feel all warm and fuzzy. This may sound eccentric, but even physicists agree that energy is constant—the law of conservation of energy states that energy can neither be created nor destroyed; rather, it can only transform from one form to another. Whether good or bad, this energy is invisible, but just because we can't see it doesn't mean that it's not out there, attaching itself to us.

Witches believe that it is very important to find out as much as possible about the food we eat *before* we eat it. Generally, most of us are quite content with visiting the supermarket and filling up our shopping carts each week to feed our families and ourselves. We are lucky to have such a wide selection of foods produced from the four corners of the globe. Today we can purchase endless vegetables that are not necessarily in season, we have herbs and spices from faraway countries at our fingertips, and we can pick and choose which meats to eat on a daily basis. It is wonderfully convenient—however, one big thing to consider while you are piling that shopping cart high is this: Where does the food come from? When we buy prewashed, pre-packaged lettuce, all we see is a clean plastic carton filled with fresh produce. When we buy meat, though, we often have very little idea of how the animal lived, how or where it was slaughtered, or whether it suffered any stress at the end of its life.

Although witches are by no means saints and often indulge in prepackaged foods, most like to source local meats and produce and tend to opt for organic foods when possible. Unfortunately, organic produce does cost more. If you have a garden or have access to a community garden, then know that nurturing your own produce will hep your craft. If you do not have a place to grow produce, try to support your local farmers by buying directly from them. We understand that not everyone has the time, money, or opportunity to be able to live this way, but if you can, you will find that you will feel healthier and more spiritually balanced. You really do not need vast space to grow and tend to your own vegetables, nor do you need to put too much physical energy into the upkeep of plants. Many foods eaten daily can be successfully grown in tubs on the patio or crammed quite happily into a small space. Leafy greens and herbs grow well in pots, and even potatoes and carrots can be grown in sacks!

A proper diet and good nutrition are the keys to living longer. We need food to survive and to thrive, so it is vital that we take the time to investigate as much as we possibly can into the foods we eat.

Diet Motivation Spell

In this busy world we live in, with fast-food eateries on almost every street corner, it is nearly impossible not to be tempted into eating delicious but unhealthy foods. Many of us struggle with our weight and have difficulty resisting the ease of prepackaged meals. From a spiritual perspective, self-control is often related to spiritual purification, so many witches like to cast a spell, not to necessarily have a figure like a supermodel but more to help with the motivation for weight loss and the cultivation of a healthy relationship with food.

Here is a spell that can help motivate your weight loss. It requires a tumbled mineral crystal called *apatite*; if you can't find one in a store that sells spiritual objects, it's easy to find one online. Just as its name describes, this gem is thought to control the appetite and help ease cravings.

Materials

1 apatite crystal

Photograph of yourself at your healthiest weight

1 length of red ribbon (giftwrapping style is fine)

Ritual

The moon phase is very important for this spell, so begin your ritual on the night of a waxing moon, a phase that is wonderful for dispelling bad habits and getting rid of things or circumstances that cause us to lose control.

Take the photograph and place the crystal on top of it. Next, fold the photograph around the crystal and tie the folded parcel closed with a red ribbon. (Red represents passion and desire as well as the fire element, so this color will help fire up your motivation to diet.) Place the package outside under the waxing moon overnight (or on a windowsill in the moonlight) to soak up the moon's magickal rays. Retrieve it the next morning and then keep it on your person every day. Each time you get a food craving, remove the stone from the parcel, lie down, and place it on your solar plexus chakra.

Spell to Feel Fuller

This spell will make you feel fuller for longer and automatically make you add less food to your plate.

Materials

1 ginseng root

1 dandelion tea bag

1 cup (240 ml) bottled spring water

   Small pot

1 cinnamon stick

1 length of red ribbon (giftwrapping style is fine)

1 yellow candle

Ritual:

Place the ginseng root, dandelion tea bag, cinnamon stick, and spring water in a small pot. All of these ingredients are superb for magickally helping weight loss. (Other foods that can aid in weight loss are ginger, cayenne pepper, mustard, turmeric, and black pepper.) Simmer for 2–3 minutes, then remove from the heat.

Take out the tea bag and the cinnamon stick and allow the potion to cool. Place the red ribbon (again for motivation) and the cooled pot beside the yellow candle. Light the candle and say the following spell twelve times, with intent:

"Less food on my plate will help my weight,
This potion will banish the cravings I hate,
I take control, I'm happy within,
Self-assured, slim and trim."

When you have recited the spell, close the ritual by saying the words "so mote it be."

Transfer the entire potion from the pot into a plastic screw-top bottle and place it in the fridge. Every morning while you are on the diet, take a sip of the potion and say the above spell once. If you feel like you are getting a craving for something you shouldn't be eating, have another sip of the liquid and repeat as above. For a bit of extra magick, snip the red ribbon into small sections. Place a piece of the ribbon in your fridge, your car, or anywhere you might be tempted to eat when you shouldn't. It is a good idea to have a little piece in your purse, too, to stop you from buying food impulsively. This ribbon will boost your motivation and stop you from giving in to those cravings.

Note: If you find the potion is a little bitter to the taste, you can add one teaspoon of locally sourced honey to the boiling liquid the next time you make it.

THE WITCH'S MOON-BASED DIET

Some witches like to take complete control of their diets and eat according to the moon's phases. Because so many of us now focus on eating healthily, this practice is becoming more popular with each year. The moon is known to rule tides, which in turn affect our body's internal chemistry and our mood swings.

The first twenty-four hours of a moon phase is when the following eating plans should be implemented. Always check with your health-care practitioner before starting any diet.

The Full Moon and the New Moon

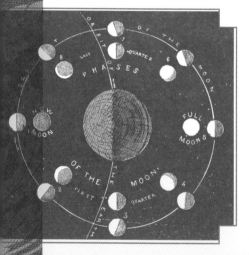

The first twenty-four hours of a full or new moon—both are times for new beginnings and cleansing—are the best times for fasting. (*Note: Although scientifically a moon phase only lasts an instant because the moon is continuously orbiting the earth, to the naked eye, the new and full phases seem to last about three days—we will consider a phase to be three days for our purposes.*) A short spell of fasting is thought to be very good not only for the body but also to bring clarity to the mind and soul. It helps us to focus on what is important and center ourselves into a deeper understanding of spirituality. No solid foods are allowed during this time—only pure water and herbal teas, which help with the detoxification process. Green tea, mint tea, and chamomile tea are perfect for cleansing the body and ridding it of all toxins. Some witches prefer to brew tea from dandelion, lemon, or sage, but any herbal tea will suffice.

For the next two days of the full-moon or new-moon phase, you can happily go back to solid food, but keep your diet rich in vegetables and limit meat. If you must eat meat, eat lean proteins like fish and chicken. Otherwise, stick to nonmeat sources of protein, like nuts, beans, soy, and quinoa. A cup of herbal tea should be consumed every night before bed and no snacks should be consumed after 6:00 p.m. This simple detoxification process will help shed excess water in the body.

The Waning Crescent Moon and the Waxing Gibbous Moon

Feasting in time with the phases of the moon can also be beneficial. If you feast during the first twenty-four hours of the waning crescent phase (before a new moon), you can banish bad forces from your life. Feasting before a waxing gibbous phase (before a full moon) can help you grow and overcome obstacles. The options below list different choices you have for how to eat during the first twenty-four hours of either of these moon phases. Eat as much as you like during the twenty-four hour period—no need to feel hungry! If you follow a feast with a fast, both spells become more powerful.

- Eat only in-season fruits, such as apples, oranges, peaches, plums, or berries that are easily sourced from your surrounding locality. These can be eaten whole or whizzed up in juicers to create smoothies.
- Eat only boiled vegetables of any kind or salads made with raw vegetables, such as lettuce, cucumber, tomatoes, onions, beets, or potatoes. For each meal, make sure you limit each portion to either all cooked or all uncooked vegetables. For example, don't eat raw cucumbers with cooked potatoes.
- Eat only cooked (boiled, baked, or grilled) root vegetables, such as pumpkins, gourds, potatoes, carrots, turnips, and parsnips.
- Eat only soups prepared from fresh, seasonal vegetables; use the vegetables to make soup stocks.

COOK UP SOME MAGICK

Cooking and preparing your food from scratch using locally sourced and seasonal produce is the best way to ensure a healthy lifestyle. Cooking is an enjoyable part of life that some, although not all, relish. Preparing and cooking food with the right intent will transport magick onto the plate, and that will not only bless the meal but also the people consuming it. Kitchen witches like to cast simple rituals over the food while it is sizzling on the stove, so it's not unusual when venturing into a witch's kitchen to see candles burning alongside an array of spices. Here is an example of a simple, heart-warming, home-cooked magickal lunch of bread and soup.

Magickal Loaf of Bread

There's nothing more comforting than the smell of bread baking in the oven, and this magickal loaf will make everyone in the family happy.

Makes 1 loaf

Ingredients

- 1 sprig fresh rosemary, stem removed
- 1 sprig fresh oregano
- 1 sprig fresh thyme
- 4 cups (544 g) bread flour
- 1 teaspoon salt
- 1 packet instant yeast
- 2 tablespoons superfine baker's sugar
- 3 tablespoons olive oil
- 1⅓ cups (360 ml) water, or enough to bring the dough together
- 7 white candles

- Chop the herbs and mix them together in a bowl. (It is best if they are homegrown). Place each of the other ingredients in separate bowls. Light a white candle next to them. Say the following spell once:

> *"Bless this food, these magickal gifts,*
> *Our mood is bright with every bite."*

- Mix all the dried ingredients in a bowl, then make a well in the center and pour in the oil and water. Stir the ingredients together and then tip out onto a floured surface and knead for 15 minutes, stretching and pulling. While you are kneading the bread, repeat the spell above, over and over again. Through the use of your hands, you are transporting good energy into the food you are preparing.

- Grease a bowl and place the dough inside it. Cover with plastic wrap or a clean towel. Let the dough rise in a warm place for 1 hour and then punch it back and knead it for another 15 minutes. While you are kneading, say the spell over and over again. Move the bread to a greased tin and leave it to rise for another hour; meanwhile, preheat your oven to 350°F (175°C) so it will reach the desired temperature by the end of this hour. Place the dough in the oven, and bake for 20–30 minutes.

Tomato Soup for the Soul

This hearty soup is a great dish to warm the soul. When paired with the Magickal Loaf of Bread on the previous page, it becomes a powerful meal to reset your witchy self. It cleanses negativity and protects you from that which would cause you harm or ill will.

Serves 6 people

Ingredients

- 20 large plum tomatoes (sourced or grown locally), cut in half
- 2 large onions, chopped
- ½ bulb garlic, whole
- 2 bay leaves
- 1 tablespoon sugar
- 2 tablespoons olive oil

- 2 cups (475 ml) chicken or vegetable stock
- 6 sun-dried tomatoes

  Handful fresh basil leaves
- 1 teaspoon paprika

  Salt and pepper to taste
- 1 white candle

- Preheat the oven to 350°F (175°C).

- Place the plum tomatoes, onions, garlic, and bay leaves in an ovenproof dish. Sprinkle the sugar on top, then drizzle with the olive oil. Roast in the oven for 20–30 minutes or until the tomatoes start to brown.

- Remove the dish from the oven and pour the contents into a saucepan. Add the stock and bring to a boil. Simmer for 30 minutes.

- Next, add the sun-dried tomatoes to the saucepan, then the basil leaves, and then the paprika. Simmer for another 30 minutes. Remove from the heat and leave to cool for about 30 minutes.

- After the soup is cooled, pour it into a blender and puree until fine.

- Pour the soup into a clean saucepan and gently reheat, stirring it with a wooden spoon. Add salt and pepper to taste.

- As the soup is reheating, light the white candle. Once the soup is heated to the desired temperature, serve it in bowls accompanied by the Magickal Loaf of Bread. Before eating, recite this spell three times:

> *"I thank the earth, I honor this meal,*
> *Within my being, the power I feel,*
> *I share with those the blessings bestowed,*
> *Soup for the soul and magickal dough."*

- Let the candle burn throughout this magickal meal, and when you have finished eating, say the words "so mote it be."

GREEN YOUR LIFE

There are thousands of different herbs and plants that will help with general, everyday ailments. Below I have short-listed some common types that you might have kicking around in the kitchen. Depending on the type of herb or plant, it can either be included in your meals on a daily basis, or incorporated in your spell work by presenting them on your altar. Failing those options, you might prefer to go to your local herbalist and purchase some supplements.

AVOCADO Boosts sexual libido, keeps your heart healthy

BANANA Keeps your heart healthy, good for blood circulation, boosts male sex drive, boosts female fertility

BASIL Eases headaches, tension, indigestion, muscle spasms, insomnia, earaches; reduces stress on the body; improves skin

BAY Improves strength and vigor

BEET Antioxidant, great source of iron

BILBERRY Good for the brain and heart (avoid if you have diabetes or are taking medication that slows blood-clotting, such as warfarin)

BRAHMI (or Centella) Good for blood circulation (may cause drowsiness, avoid taking with sedatives or with medications that might be harmful to your liver)

BURDOCK Alleviates dandruff and acne (avoid if you are taking medication that slows blood-clotting)

CARDAMOM Eases indigestion, powerful in lusty spells, helps improve sexual problems

CATNIP Eases teething, colic, diarrhea, indigestion, anxiety, antidepressant, insomnia (may cause drowsiness, avoid taking with sedatives)

CELERY SEEDS Diuretic, eases menstrual discomfort

CHAMOMILE Eases insomnia, anxiety, stress, fever, arthritis, pain, indigestion (may decrease effectiveness of birth-control pills and some cancer medications; may increase the effects of warfarin; discuss usage with your doctor if you are taking medication for your liver)

CHOCOLATE (dark) Helps lower blood pressure, boosts mental function

CINNAMON (ground) Soothes sore throats and coughs, anti-inflammatory (avoid taking with medications for diabetes)

DANDELION Detoxifying, constipation relief/laxative (avoid if you are on antibiotics, lithium, or water pills; discuss usage with your doctor if you are taking medication for your liver)

DILL Eases menstrual discomfort, insomnia, hiccups; aids digestion

ECHINACEA Boosts immune system, wards off colds (discuss usage with your doctor if you are taking any medication that is changed by the liver)

ELDERBERRY Wards off colds and flu (avoid taking with medications that decrease the immune system)

FENUGREEK Reduces blood-sugar levels in diabetics

FEVERFEW Eases headaches and menstrual discomfort (avoid taking with medications for diabetes or that slow blood-clotting)

FIGS Boosts fertility

GARLIC Boosts cardiovascular system

GINGER Eases morning sickness, nausea, colic, indigestion, diarrhea, fever, sore throats (avoid taking with medication that slows blood-clotting)

GINSENG Aphrodisiac, mild stimulant, boosts immune system (do *not* take with medications for diabetes or that slow blood-clotting, or with MAO inhibitors)

HORSERADISH ROOT Expectorant, eases stuffy nose; used in exorcisms

IVY Placed on altars during healing rituals to intensify spell potency

JASMINE Keeps away night terrors, makes dreaming peaceful

JUNIPER Boosts all-around health (avoid taking with medication for diabetes)

KNOTWEED Placed on altar for general health spells

LEMON BALM Eases anxiety, cold sores, colic, insomnia, restlessness, indigestion; memory booster (may cause drowsiness, avoid taking with sedative medications)

LICORICE Eases heartburn and itchy skin (do *not* take with medications that slow blood-clotting; interacts with numerous medications, discuss usage with your doctor)

MILK THISTLE Eases heartburn (discuss with your doctor if you are taking any medications that are changed by the liver)

NETTLE Eases hay fever and arthritis, diuretic (avoid taking with medications for diabetes, high blood pressure, or that slow blood-clotting; sedatives; or lithium)

OATS Helps lower cholesterol; magickally improve potency and fertility

OLIVES Helps bone health

PARSLEY Rich in iron (do *not* take with medications that slow blood-clotting or with diuretics)

PASSIONFLOWER Eases anxiety, may help tired eyes (may cause drowsiness, avoid taking with sedatives)

PEPPER (black or white, ground) Aids digestion, stimulates taste buds

QUINCE (fruit) Helps gastrointestinal inflammation, healthy skin (do *not* take with any oral medications, as their effectiveness may be decreased; avoid if pregnant or breastfeeding, as the seeds contain trace amounts of cyanide)

RADISH Detoxifying

ROSEHIPS Eases stiffness from osteoarthritis (do not take with antacids, estrogen, lithium, fluphenazine, or medications that slow blood-clotting)

ROSEMARY Improves focus, memory, concentration, blood pressure, circulation; antiseptic, antidepressant; eases indigestion

SAGE Enhances mental function and memory, helps menopausal symptoms, can be used as an antiseptic mouthwash (avoid taking with sedatives, or with medications for diabetes or seizure prevention)

TOMATO Prosperity, protection, love

THYME Antibacterial, antiseptic, expectorant; eases coughs and colds (do *not* take with medications that slow blood-clotting)

TURMERIC Anti-inflammatory, reduces cholesterol

VALERIAN Eases insomnia (do *not* take with alcohol, sedatives, or anti-anxiety medications)

WILLOW BARK Natural aspirin, eases general aches and pains (do *not* take with aspirin, ibuprofen, or medications that slow blood-clotting)

Color Properties in Food

Our planet is full of beautiful and amazing herbs, vegetables, fruits, and spices. We have calming chamomile, spicy chili peppers, and warming ginger. Including a wide variety of these ingredients in our diets can only do us good. Medical science tells us that colorful foods have massive health benefits and are full of vitamins, minerals, fiber, and phytochemicals, which are believed to act as antioxidants. These are called superfoods, and you should try to incorporate a few of them into your weekly diet. Eat greens like spinach, kale, and broccoli; blues and purples like eggplant, blackberries, and blueberries; reds like chilies, beets, and tomatoes; and oranges like cantaloupe, sweet potatoes, and squash. Also, don't rule out the occasional glass of red wine!

SABBATS AND HOLIDAYS FEASTS
WITCHES SHARE THEIR FAVORITE
HOLIDAY TREATS

Charity Bedell's Tourtière (Meat Pie)

This family recipe is for a pork-based pie that is perfect for Yule and Christmas. Pork was often eaten and sacrificed at Yule to the Norse god Freyr. My family typically serves this on Christmas day for breakfast.

Serves 6 to 8

Ingredients

$\frac{1}{2}$ tablespoon butter or olive oil

1 pound (450 g) ground pork

2 medium-to-large onions, diced

Salt, pepper, and cinnamon to taste

2 potatoes of any type, boiled or microwaved to softness, then mashed

Pie crust top and bottom (store-bought is fine)

Mustard to taste if desired

- Grease a large, deep pan with butter or olive oil. Sauté the meat, onions, and spices together in the pan and simmer, covered, for 2 hours on medium-to-low heat, stirring frequently.

- Meanwhile, preheat the oven to 375°F (190°C).

- Add cooked potatoes to the meat mixture and loosely fold in.

- Place the bottom pie crust in an ungreased glass pie-baking dish. Fill with the meat-and-potato mixture. Cover with the top crust, using a fork to seal the two crusts together. Place the pie in the oven and bake for 25 minutes or until golden brown. Serve warm, with mustard on top if desired.

Shawn Robbins's After-Dinner Holiday Treat

This smoothie is delicious, fun to make, and good for your health. The dash of alcohol makes it a festive dessert treat for Lughnasadh (see page 263), when fresh berries are in season. (But you can have it on other holidays, too, and this recipe can be made with fresh or frozen fruit.)

Serves 2 to 3

Ingredients

½ cup (100 g) strawberries

½ cup (50 g) blueberries

½ cup (65 g) raspberries

1 banana

1 cup (250 g) flavored yogurt (any flavor you like)

1 tablespoon vanilla

½ cup (120 ml) pineapple juice

8 ice cubes

- Magickal ingredient: a shot of your favorite fruit-flavored liquor, for added sweetness (I recommend cherry vodka).

- Place all of the ingredients in a blender, and blend on high until the mixture is smooth. Drink up and enjoy!

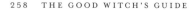

Melodie Starr Ball's Halloween Pumpkin Bread

Halloween is one of the most magickal nights of the year! It is the night when a witch's power is strongest and when the veil between this world and the other side is thinnest. The original reason for Halloween was, among other things, to celebrate the circle of life by honoring those who have passed away. On Halloween, we invite our dead ancestors to celebrate their lives with us and have a feast with candles, games, and sweets (Halloween parties). Some traditional food for a Halloween feast includes apples, pears, pumpkin pie, corn, cider, and meat. There is a tradition of burning hazel or pine incense and white sage to keep any negative spirits from entering your home.

Many people hold séances because it is much easier to make contact with the other side at this time. With a witch's powers spiking on this night, it is a good time to perform divination rituals. Whether you use tarot, water scrying, or another type of divination, any spell or ritual performed on Halloween night is sure to be a great success! Many people have bonfires on Halloween night. Some say this is to keep ghosts and goblins away; however, fire scrying, or divining the future by gazing into open flames, is another form of divination that is very effective.

Following is a recipe that my grandmother always made for our Halloween parties:

Makes 2 loaves

Ingredients

3½ cups (448 g) all-purpose flour

2 teaspoons baking powder

1 teaspoon ground allspice

1 teaspoon ground cinnamon

1 teaspoon ground nutmeg (which adds to a witch's power!)

¾ teaspoon salt

½ teaspoon baking soda

½ teaspoon ground cloves

1⅓ cups (290 g) packed brown sugar, plus ½ cup (110 g) or more to taste

¾ cup (180 ml) milk

½ cup (120 ml) vegetable oil

2 teaspoons vanilla extract

2 large eggs

1 15-ounce can pumpkin puree

Cooking spray

⅓ cup (40 g) chopped walnuts

- Preheat the oven to 350°F (175°C).

- Mix the flour, baking powder, allspice, cinnamon, nutmeg, salt, baking soda, and cloves in a large bowl; make a well in center of mixture. In a separate bowl, whisk together the brown sugar, milk, vegetable oil, vanilla, eggs, and pumpkin puree in a bowl. Pour into the well of the flour mixture and stir just until moist.

- Coat 2 loaf pans with cooking spray, and spoon the batter into the coated pans. Sprinkle with the walnuts. Bake for 1 hour or until a wooden toothpick inserted in the center comes out clean. Cool loaves in pans on a wire rack for 10 minutes, then remove from pans. Sprinkle a little brown sugar on top. Cool loaves completely before serving.

Derrie P. Carpenter's Three-Ingredient Yule Shortbread Cookies

Yule is the pagan version of Christmas, and it is also the recognition of the winter solstice. In my family, we celebrate both Yule and Christmas, as we live in a mixed-religion household. Yule is my favorite Sabbat, and it means family, love, and magick to me. We do as much as we can by candlelight, as this Sabbat is also a fire Sabbat, because it marks the rebirth of the sun.

Yule can be celebrated many different ways. The most common way I have come across is with a Yule log. Each species of tree is imbued with different magickal and spiritual properties. You can choose the type of wood that is right for you and your family: oak for strength; aspen for protection and spirituality; birch for fertility; pine for purification and prosperity.

Before the Yule log is burned, it is decorated and displayed, often as a beautiful centerpiece for a holiday meal. Decorations can include candles, mistletoe, holly, cranberries, and cloth or paper ribbon. My favorite thing about the Yule holiday, though, is the tradition in my family to bake shortbread cookies!

Makes approximately 15 cookies

Ingredients

- 1 cup (2 sticks, or 227 g) butter, softened
- ½ cup (60 g) confectioners' sugar
- 2 cups (240 g) all-purpose flour
- Extra flour or confectioners' sugar for dusting and rolling

- Preheat the oven to 350°F (175°C). Line two large baking sheets with parchment paper* or a silicone baking mat.

  - In a large bowl, cream together the butter and sugar. Add the flour and continue to mix until a soft dough forms (it will be crumbly at first, but keep mixing and it will form a smooth dough). With your hands, form the dough into a cohesive ball.

  - Using a rolling pin and work surface that is well dusted with flour or confectioners' sugar**, roll the dough out to a 1/4-inch (6-mm) thickness. Cut the dough into rounds and place on prepared baking sheets about a 1/2 inch (12 mm) apart. Repeat as necessary.

- Bake for 16–18 minutes or until cookies are pale golden brown. Let cool on baking sheets. Store baked cookies in a resealable container or plastic bag at room temperature for up to 4 days. Serve with tea or coffee, or use as a base for any recipe requiring shortbread.

*Note: Do not use the parchment paper with foil lining underneath, as it may make the paper curl up and over your cookies as they're baking.

**You can use either flour or powdered sugar to roll out your cookies, but I prefer powdered sugar, which keeps the cookies from becoming too dense and floury as you repeatedly roll it out. Whichever you use, remember to keep your surface and rolling pin well-dusted. If you are using powdered sugar, you may need to dust your surface and rolling pin more often than you would if you use flour.

Connie Davoie's Fry Bread for Lughnasadh

Lughnasadh—also known as Lammas, Loafmas, Lúnasa, or Pagan Thanksgiving—is one of the four cross-quarter days between the solstices and equinoxes, meaning it falls almost halfway between the summer solstice and autumn equinox. In the northern hemisphere, it starts at sunset on July 31 and goes 'til sunset of August 1, and in the southern hemisphere, it runs from January 31 to February 1. It is one of the four fire festivals and a Celtic holiday that is celebrated by many Wiccans and neo-pagans, especially those with roots in Celtic culture.

Lughnasadh is the first Sabbat of the fruits and grains, as it happens when the grains and fruits from the year's first harvest are picked, so it is normally celebrated with a feast. Hand-fasting (Wiccan wedding) ceremonies are also often held during Lughnasadh.

They say that some of our ancient ancestors would cut the first harvest corn and other grains and then go to the mountains and bury them as offerings to the gods for thanks and continued good harvests. People would come from miles around to trade, sell, and share their bounty and other goods, along with feasting on breads and cakes made from the grains of the harvest. There was dancing, drinking of ale, plenty of games, and tall tales to be told around the bonfires. . . .

Today, we can still celebrate by giving thanks to the gods, the workers, and the spirits of the earth for these gifts and for the blessings of friends and family. We can celebrate by inviting our friends, families, coworkers, and neighbors for a potluck dinner of breads, cakes, fruits, and veggies and to sit around a bonfire and tell stories.

Fry bread is another name for bannock bread, which is a traditional Celtic bread made on Lughnasadh.

Makes 8 to 12 small portions or 6 to 8 larger portions

Ingredients

3 cups (385 g) all-purpose flour

1 tablespoon baking powder

1 teaspoon salt

1¼ (300 ml) cups warm water

Extra flour for dusting and rolling

Vegetable oil, lard, or shortening,
    enough to fill your frying pan
    to a minimum of 1 inch
    (25 mm) deep

- Sift the flour thoroughly with the baking powder and salt in a mixing bowl. Make a well in the center of the flour mixture and pour the warm water into the center of the well. Work the flour mixture into the liquid with a wooden spoon or your hands. Gently knead the dough into a ball and then shape it into a 3-inch (8-cm) round cylinder. Cover the dough with a clean kitchen towel to prevent drying and let it sit for about 10 minutes. (It is best to use the dough within a few hours, although it may be used the next day if kept in a covered container or wrapped in plastic wrap, refrigerated, and then allowed to warm to room temperature before using.)

- To form the bread, place the dough on a cutting board. With a dough cutter or knife, begin halving, then quartering, etc., the cylinder of dough until you reach the desired thickness. Cut smaller slices for appetizers and larger ones for sandwiches. As you go, cover the cut slices of dough with a clean towel to prevent drying.

- Once you have cut all of your slices, it is time to roll them out. First place some flour in a shallow dish to work with while rolling out the dough. Lightly dust the slices with some of the flour. On a lightly floured work surface, use a rolling pin to roll each slice to about ¼-inch (6-mm) thickness. Place each rolled-out slice in the flour dish, turning to lightly coat and then gently shaking to remove the excess flour. Stack the finished slices on a plate as you go, and cover with a dry towel until ready to cook.

- Heat the oil (or melt the lard or shortening) in a deep, heavy pan over medium-high to about 350°F (175°C). Gently place pieces of bread in the oil—do not throw them in or overcrowd the pan. Cook 2 to 3 minutes per side until golden. Once cooked, drain on paper towels to absorb excess oil. Serve warm, and top with any of your favorites: confectioners' sugar, cinnamon and sugar, maple syrup, honey, homemade honey butter (see following recipe), or melted cheese.

Homemade Honey Butter

Makes approximately 1 cup (230 g)

Ingredients

1 pint (475 ml) of heavy cream or whipping cream

Salt (optional)

Honey to taste

- Pour a pint of heavy cream or whipping cream into a bowl or into a jar with a tight-fitting lid. You can either use a hand-mixer or shake a jar by hand to form the butter. If using a mixer, start on low speed, then raise to medium speed. If you're using a jar, start shaking! The cream will first form soft whipped cream, then stiff peaks. Keep going until the cream breaks into clumps. If you're shaking the cream by hand, you will feel the liquid thickening and begin to see it solidifying after about 10 to 20 minutes; if you're using a mixer, the butter will start to cling to the beaters after about 5 to 10 minutes. Make sure you don't overbeat the mixture, because it will turn back to liquid if this happens.

- Remove the butter from the jar or bowl, and strain the remaining liquid through cheesecloth. (This is buttermilk, which you can save for other things or give to your pet as a treat.) Place the butter in a container or bowl; add salt and honey to taste.

Sweet Banana Bread for Ostara by Sherry, aka Phoenix Rayn Song

I've been a practicing Wiccan witch for many years, and during my life I've had two defining and momentous occasions. The first was the birth of my incredible son twenty years ago, and the second was when I was initiated as a high priestess. Those incredible moments of change are in my thoughts today as we consider one of our spring Sabbats, Ostara.

Ostara is celebrated on the spring (vernal) equinox. "Equinox" comes from the Latin *aequinoctium*, meaning "equal night." With the sun directly above the equator, day and night are almost equal. This equality signals that change is near. The days will get longer, the temperatures will get warmer, and the earth will come out of her peaceful winter slumber. These celestial and terrestrial occurrences usher in the changes in nature, life, and spirit that we as Wiccans enjoy and celebrate at springtime.

Spiritually speaking, spring is the season of new beginnings, fertility, and growth. The name *Ostara* is derived from the Germanic goddess Eostre—goddess of the dawn, spring, and fertility and an ultimate example of life's changing ways. . . . Eostre is associated with blooming flowers and bunny rabbits, two very traditional symbols of fecundity, as well as decorated fertility eggs. . . .

Today, the Wiccan celebration of Ostara occurs outside, where we can enjoy nature's changes, feel the warm sun, see animals courting, and smell the fresh newness of the earth. . . .

I tend to spend Ostara day out in my yard watching the birds, enjoying the budding flowers, and searching for telltale signs of new life. I decorate my altar with flowers, painted eggs, and rabbit statues and create a special treat as an offering to Eostre. One of my favorite things to make is a little loaf of banana bread, as it tastes and smells so incredible. It adds sweetness to my offering, and fresh blooms can be laid upon the top of the batter as it's baking. Below is my sweet banana bread recipe if you would like to give it a try.

Makes 1 loaf

Ingredients

- ½ cup (113 g) unsalted butter, softened
- 1 cup (200 g) sugar
- ¾ teaspoon salt
- 1 teaspoon baking soda
- ½ teaspoon vanilla
- 2 eggs
- ½ cup (120 ml) milk with 1 tablespoon vinegar added
- 2 cups (680 g) mashed banana

- Cream butter and sugar in a bowl until fluffy. Stir in salt, baking soda, vanilla, and eggs, and then beat in milk-and-vinegar mixture and bananas. Bake in a greased bread pan for 60 minutes at 350°F (175°C).

Cheryl Croce Culver's Cinnamon Muffins for Beltane

Merry meet. When I think of the Sabbat of Beltane, I think about May baskets, trees budding out into new growth after the long winter months, and spring flowers popping forth from the frozen ground and showing us that warmth and sunshine are returning to the earth. The name *Beltane* comes from the Celtic word "Bel-fire," or "fire of the Celtic god Bel" (also called Beli, Balar, Balor, Belenus), god of light and fire. Beltane is a time of bonfires to welcome warmth and a time for new life and fertility. It is a festival of flowers, sensuality, and delight. Everything is coming awake, and the cycle of life once again begins. Love is in the air, and it is a time to run and play and get out of our homes to seek food and fun. We have spring fever!

The most memorable and obvious symbol of Beltane is the maypole. A phallic symbol, it represents the male, stimulating force in nature, and it is used to show the sacred union between the goddess and god that takes place at this time. The pole represents the god, of course, and the earth around the pole represents the goddess. . . .

Beltane is associated with dairy and breads, and these muffins are one of my favorite Beltane recipes.

Makes 12 muffins

Ingredients

½ cup (64 g) all-purpose flour

½ cup (100 g) sugar

2 teaspoons baking powder

½ teaspoon sea salt

½ teaspoon ground nutmeg

¼ teaspoon ground allspice

½ teaspoon cinnamon

1 egg, beaten

½ cup (120 ml) milk

⅓ cup (76 g) butter, melted

Topping

2 tablespoons sugar

½ teaspoon ground cinnamon

¼ cup (57 g) butter, melted

- Mix flour, sugar, baking powder, salt, nutmeg, allspice, and cinnamon. Stir egg, milk, and butter into dry ingredients until moistened. Spoon batter into greased or paper-lined muffin cups. Bake at 400°F (205°C) for 20 minutes or until a wooden toothpick inserted into the center of a muffin comes out clean.

- For topping, combine the sugar and cinnamon. Brush the tops of the warm muffins with the melted butter and dip them into the sugar-and-cinnamon mixture.

Katie Snow's Honey-Lemon Shortbread Cookies for Litha

Litha, also known as midsummer, is centered around the summer solstice, the longest day of the year. The exact dates vary by where you are geographically, but the holiday is typically celebrated between June 19 and June 25. The celebration of Midsummer's Eve, which predates Christianity, was the festival of the summer solstice. During these festivals, large bonfires were set to ward off the evil spirits that were believed to roam the earth freely while the sun turned toward the south. Astrologically at this time, the sun is entering Cancer, so midsummer is not only a great time for fire magick but also water magick. This is a good time for honoring the Oak King by having oak leaves and all the colors of summer on your altar.

Litha is a time to get back to nature as the fields grow and flowers bloom. Try to spend as much time as you can outdoors, enjoying the sun that is once again warming the earth. A perfect way to celebrate is a bonfire and get-together with family and friends to share summertime fare. Litha is a joyous time of the year, full of all the fun that the summer months have to offer. Adding a drum circle or music and dancing to your celebration is a wonderful way to fully enjoy any midsummer gathering.

These delightful cookies are a summertime favorite for my family. Full of flavor with just enough sweetness, they are a flavorful addition to any celebration.

Makes about 45 cookies

Ingredients

3 3/4 cups (480 g) all-purpose flour

1/2 teaspoon salt

1/4 teaspoon baking powder

1 1/2 cups (3 sticks, or 340 g) unsalted butter, at room temperature

3/4 cup (165 g) packed brown sugar

1/2 teaspoon of lemon emulsion

1 teaspoon lemon zest

1/4 cup (85 g) honey, plus 2–3 tablespoons for brushing cookies

Turbinado sugar for sprinkling on cookies

- Combine flour, salt, and baking powder. Set aside. In a separate bowl, beat together butter and sugar until light in color and fluffy. Add honey, lemon emulsion, and lemon zest, and beat until it is just combined. Scrape sides of bowl as necessary.

- Gradually add flour mixture to the honey-lemon mixture, and continue to mix until just combined into dough. Move dough onto a large sheet of wax or parchment paper and shape into a long, skinny log about 2 inches (50 mm) in diameter. Roll up the dough log in parchment or wax paper and freeze overnight until you are ready to bake the next day.

- When you're ready to bake the cookies, preheat oven to 350°F (175°C). Take the dough out of the freezer and cut 1/4-inch (6-mm) thick slices. Place the slices on baking sheets lined with parchment paper.

- Heat 2–3 tablespoons of honey in the microwave for 10–15 seconds. Brush the honey over the cookies and immediately sprinkle them with turbinado sugar. Bake for 10–12 minutes or until just golden brown. Do not overbake. Let cool for about 5 minutes on baking sheets before removing the cookies from the sheets and placing them on a cooling rack. Once fully cooled, store in an airtight container.

Dori Hayes's, aka Darklady's, Mabon Sausage Soup

Mabon, to me, means the first day of fall, when the days and nights are the same length and winter will soon be here. Mabon—celebrated at the autumnal equinox, the midpoint between harvesting and sowing crops—is when we should give thanks as well as look back on the past year and plan for the coming one.

Mabon is also a time of rest and celebration, a time for spells of protection, prosperity, security, and self-confidence. The colors to use are gold, orange, yellow, red, bronze, and rust. I set up an altar indoors using a small, round table. On my altar are acorns and leaves that I have collected, along with corn. I also cut apples down the middle, so I can see the seeds in their star shape, and then I dry them and string them with pinecones in between—it's very pretty. I lay those on the altar, too. I light a yellow-and-orange candle and ask for blessings to come into my life and for peace in the world.

Then it's time to fix my Mabon meal, sausage soup—it's wicked good. After we all sit down and give thanks to the goddess and eat, I always go for a walk in the woods or by the river—not only to walk off the dinner, but also so I can breathe and be closer to nature.

Blessings to all of you.

Serves 6 to 8

Ingredients

- 3   sausages (I like it with a kick, so I use hot sausage)
- 3   medium white onions
- 3   large cans kidney beans
- 3   large cans stewed, chopped tomatoes
- 8   small Yukon Gold potatoes
-      Bay leaf, thyme, and garlic powder to taste
-      Salt and pepper to taste

- Heat the sausage and onions in a large soup pot until very well cooked. Add the other ingredients, and simmer until potatoes are tender. Serve in a bowl with your favorite French or sourdough bread.

Rachel McGirr's Imbolc Cake

Imbolc is an important feast day in the Celtic tradition. It marks the point between the winter solstice and the spring equinox. It's a time of rebirth and hope that begins to stir in the long-awaited return of the spring. Here in Ireland, where it is also known as *Oimelc*, celebratory Gaelic festivals are held all over the country from sunrise to sunset.

Corn dollies, Brigid's crosses, and corn cakes are made from the grains, reeds of straw, and wheat that were gathered at the harvest.

Imbolc was considered one of the cornerstones in the traditional Celtic calendar, because, as the winter stores of produce were getting really low, the success of the new farming season was of great importance. The name *Imbolc* comes from the old Irish *imblog*, meaning "in the belly," which is a reference to pregnant ewes and milking. Imbolc rituals took place in order to harness the divine energy that would help the farmers grow a good supply of produce until the next harvest, which takes place six months later.

In Ireland, Imbolc also celebrates the triple goddess Brigid, who represents the chronological stages of the maiden, mother, and crone. Brigid is celebrated on the eves of January 31 and March 1 at the Mound of the Hostages on the Hill of Tara, a megalithic tomb in County Meath, Ireland, where, on those days, the rising sun aligns with the inner chamber. The lighting of fires celebrates the ever-increasing power of the sun over the coming month.

This is a recipe for my Imbolc cake; you can prepare and bake this cake all in one baking tin!

Ingredients

1 3/4 cups (224 g) all-purpose flour

1/2 cup (100 g) sugar

2 tablespoons poppy seeds

1 tablespoon baking soda

1/2 tablespoon salt

3/4 cup (180 ml) water

1/4 cup (60 ml) vegetable oil

1 tablespoon lemon peel

1 tablespoon orange peel

2 tablespoons lemon juice

2 tablespoons orange juice

Powdered sugar

· Preheat oven to 350°F (175°C). Mix flour, sugar, poppy seeds, baking soda, and salt with a fork in an ungreased 9 × 9 × 2–inch (23 × 23 × 5–cm) baking tin. Stir in the remaining ingredients except the powdered sugar. Bake for 35–40 minutes or until a wooden toothpick inserted into the center comes out clean and the top is golden brown. Remove from the oven and let cool. Sprinkle with powdered sugar.

Pass It Along

The beauty of Wicca is that there are no hard-and-fast rules, so you can explore all the rituals and recipes discussed in this chapter and pursue only those that you feel most drawn to . . . and then share them. This is, after all, how traditions and beliefs are carried on, passed down through the ages, and maybe (depending on your skills and dedication) even improved upon.

Sabbat Wish Powder to Attract Good Fortune

BY RACHEL MCGIRR

Whatever the Sabbat, every witch knows that these are celebratory times to give thanks in the Wiccan calendar. Today, witches across the world believe that the Sabbats hold a great power and cast spells to replenish the good things in life for the months ahead. Many witches make wish powder during Sabbats so that they have something on hand should they need it in a hurry.

Wish powder works for any desire, as long as it's not greed. It's very general but does come in handy when you want to cast some magick quickly.

Materials

- **1** tall, white tapered candle with candleholder

- **3** teaspoons dried meadowsweet (a Lammas herb for luck that can be purchased online)

- **3** teaspoons dried basil, plus **3** teaspoons dried mint (a magickal blend to attract good fortune)

- Mortar and pestle

- **1** small pot of silver glitter to add to the magick and represent wishes

- **1** small plastic container with a snap-on lid

Ritual

On one of the evenings during the Sabbat you are celebrating, light the candle and place it in the candleholder. Grind the herbs as finely as you can using a pestle and mortar. Then add the small pot of glitter, and mix in well. Transfer the mixture to the plastic container and seal the lid. Hold the container in one hand and the candle in the other, and say these words seven times:

> "Magickal powder in this dish,
> Be ever powerful, grant my wish."

Leave the powder next to the candle for a couple of hours and then snuff the candle out. Store the powder under your altar or with your other magickal tools. In the coming months, when you want to make a wish, bring the wish powder outside at night.

Take a pinch of the powder and throw it into the night while silently making your wish. Be realistic with your wishes, and they should come to fruition.

Appendix

Round Table of Folk Remedies

VOICES FROM AROUND THE WORLD

From what witches know best to what pagans know best to what druids, Celts, and holistic healers and practitioners have always known—alternative medicines have worked for thousands of years.

Today, many top medical practitioners agree that, when you can't find the right medicine for what ails the patient, sometimes you have to change course and look in another direction. The answer is often out there if you only know where to find it.

Got a headache? There is an herb for that! Got a tummy problem? There is a spice for that! Got a sinus problem? There is a potion for that! Got a cold or flu? There is a brew for that!

Chamomile tea calms your nerves, peppermint oil gives you energy, volcano-ash shampoo dries up oily hair, lavender oil helps you fall asleep—one doesn't have to look far to see the magick of what your kitchen cupboard, grocery store, and nutritional center has on the shelf.

$\mathcal{A}$ffirmations and $\mathcal{A}$ttitude

BY CHARISSA

Whenever I have a medical issue—an ache, a pain, etc.—in addition to whatever medical or holistic treatment I am using for physical symptoms, I like to address the emotions that may be contributing to the issue, as well as the emotional fallout of not feeling well physically.

One of the ways I do that is with affirmations: positive statements designed to help your mind create change. Always use positive statements. Stay away from words like "no," "not," "won't," "can't," and "don't." Make your affirmations short statements of fact, not action. Repeat them many times throughout the day to bring your subconscious into agreement. Example: "I *am* happy," not "I *will be* happy" or "I *won't be* un happy."

I have found that changing my state of mind will often bring about the physical change more quickly and make the healing process easier.

HOLISTIC A-TO-Z HEALTH REMEDIES

Often we find ourselves in unexpected situations when we become ill or injured—maybe it is a holiday and the stores are all closed, or it is the middle of the night. Here are some home remedies and tips from contributors from around the globe to help keep you on the road to wellness. We want to thank our contributors for sharing their knowledge and personal stories in this chapter. You are the light in the darkness helping to illuminate the way to wellness and good health for others.

> NOTE: Always check with your health-care practitioner before taking or following any home remedy, and refer to the lists of herbs in Chapter 7 (see pages 198–200 and 205–207), which include cautions and contraindications for certain conditions. Also, as mentioned previously, for any topical treatments, always test first on a small patch of skin and wait a day to make sure you do not have any allergic reactions. Stop use if redness, swelling, or itching occurs or worsens. Also note that some of the entries here have been adapted or edited down slightly.

ACID REFLUX Chianne Frasure

Ginger has long been known as one of the best natural remedies for digestion issues. Ginger contains enzymes that stimulate your digestive system; speeding up the digestion process helps prevent the buildup of gas. It is also known for relieving nausea and vomiting, and its anti-inflammatory properties reduce inflammation and irritation. Some types of acid reflux can be treated by drinking ginger-root tea. Boil one cup (240 ml) of water in a small pot. Take a 1-inch (25-mm) slice of peeled ginger root and mince finely. Add the minced ginger to the boiling water. Boil for another five minutes, then remove from the heat and let it steep for twenty minutes.

Strain out the ginger, then stir in ½ teaspoon of honey and lemon juice to taste. Drink two times a day before each meal while symptoms last.

ALLERGIES AND SINUS ISSUES

Lashette Williams

You can oil away those allergies and sinus issues! For the general allergy sufferer who either finds that regular use of allergy medications don't help that much, there are two essential oils that I have found to help relieve many sinus issues. The first is eucalyptus oil, which has decongestant properties that relieve runny noses, stuffiness, or even sinus headaches. Second, for a sinus infection, I recommend tea tree oil. Its strong odor helps break through the stuffiness much quicker than eucalyptus, and its antiseptic properties help break down the infection.

With either oil, add a few drops to a pot of boiled water or an oil warmer for steam inhalation, or put a few drops on a hot towel or compress for sinus-headache relief. Some people even mix it with coconut oil, shea butter, or almond oil to rub on the sinus region of your face. I personally like adding eucalyptus oil or tea tree oil to a warm bath.

ALLERGIES, ANTIBACTERIAL, PH BALANCE Dru Ann Welch

"Honeygar" is Dru Ann's favorite cure-all. It is a simple combination of two very powerful substances: honey and apple cider vinegar. What is so special about this combination? Honey on its own is a strong antibacterial, and it is believed that if you use local honey (from bees in your community) it can act as an anti-allergen. Apple cider vinegar is also an antibacterial and works to balance the pH in your system. Together they pack a one-two punch to fight off infections.

To make: Take an empty jar, and fill it halfway with honey and the rest of the way with apple cider vinegar. Seal the jar and shake to mix. Take one tablespoon in the morning and one in the evening at the start of your allergies (it is also good for a cold) and continue for five to ten days.

ANXIETY Tracie (Sage) Wood

Essential oils—such as the following calming blend—can help reduce or manage mild anxiety and depression.

In a small mason jar or bottle, combine 6 drops lavender, 4 drops frankincense, 4 drops mugwort, 3 drops geranium, and 2 drops chamomile in ⅛ cup (30 ml) of a carrier oil, such as grapeseed, almond, or apricot kernel oil. (See pages 53–54 for instructions on blending, shaking, and storing the oil.) Rub the blend on your pulse points, shoulder blades, and the base of your neck as needed to manage your symptoms.

BAD BREATH Yancy Walker

I'm going to talk to you about something that nobody will tell you that you have: bad breath, or halitosis. There are several things that can cause bad breath. Chief among them is hygiene, which is very important for keeping your mouth clean and your breath fresh. Brush and floss your teeth as often as you can. I brush my teeth with a mix of hydrogen peroxide and baking soda. I used to see my mother do this when I was little, and it really grossed me out thinking about peroxide in my mouth. However, I've come to find it really doesn't have any flavor at all, and the baking soda tastes like salt. Using this combination not only helps your teeth become whiter over time but also keeps your breath fresh. The hydrogen peroxide cleans bacteria from your mouth and doesn't have the nasty taste that over-the-counter mouthwashes have. Just make sure you rinse with water afterward. I haven't used toothpaste (or mouthwash) for years, and this combination costs less.

It's important to keep saliva in your mouth, as a dry mouth also causes bad breath. One way to do this is with lemon or tart candies. Peppermint oil is also a good way to combat bad breath as well as stomach problems, which can also cause halitosis. After eating something strong (like garlic or onions), it's always good to take peppermint oil, chew on some fresh parsley or cloves, and drink plenty of water. Tobacco products cause bad breath, so if you smoke, try to stop.

BOILS Kimberlie Miller Clark
I am a third-generation healer. My grandmother Marie Miley Hughes—we called her Dr. Granny—made her own remedies. My mother, Nadine Hughes Miller, could take the pain out of a burn simply by blowing on it and rubbing it. Not too long ago, I had a relative suffering with a boil. I did some research and found a successful way to get rid of it. I hope this remedy, which originated in India, will work for you also. You'll need one root of raw turmeric, a little water, and a coarse, flat stone mortar. Boil the turmeric root in a small pot of water for fifteen minutes. Remove the root from the water, let it cool, and then rub it against the stone until it becomes a paste. Spread the paste on the boil at night and cover with gauze. Rinse the paste off with water in the morning. This should make the boil mature and drain more quickly. Do this twice a week until the boil is gone.

BRITTLE NAILS Dr. Kimberly S. McAfee
I have personally struggled with brittle nails and am happy to share a few tips I have found to help fix them! Brittle nails can be caused by dryness, so moisturizing oils and butters can be beneficial. Try natural oils like coconut or vitamin E oil, or even cocoa or shea butter—the latter is my personal favorite—and massage into the nail area. Another way to strengthen your nails is by taking herbal supplements. A great herb to try is horsetail. Horsetail has many medicinal uses, with strengthening brittle nails being one of them. It can be purchased in various forms and is inexpensive. (Note: Do not take with lithium.) An old-fashioned multivitamin accompanied with an omega-3 supplement will also help give your nails added strength. As with any herbal treatments or supplements, be sure to discuss potential usage with your healthcare practitioner in order to determine if there could be any adverse side effects.

BURNS Sunbow Pendragon
As a former restaurant professional, I have seen my share of awful burns and have treated more than a few on myself. The worst one I have ever

received was when I worked in a pizzeria in my twenties and the inside of my arm touched the side of the pizza oven. At 500 degrees, it was instantaneous pain, and I knew I had to act quickly. The first thing I did was go to the freezer and make a quick ice pack. That stopped most of the swelling and reduced the pain enough for me to finish my shift. When I got home that night, I put on aloe vera gel, which is a powerful healing agent that rehydrates the skin. I applied it thickly, letting it just soak in until I was ready for bed, then I covered it carefully with gauze to protect it while I slept. When I rose in the morning, I unwrapped it and applied more aloe gel, letting it stay open for a bit until I was ready to leave for work. I kept it dry and clean for a few days, changing out the bandage as needed, until the pain was finally gone and it looked like it was beginning to heal. I started to alternate vitamin E oil and aloe vera gel so as to avoid a serious scar. It took about two weeks before the burn was completely healed, and all the while I kept up with the vitamin E oil and aloe gel. There was never any infection. Today, I barely have a scar. Holistic treatments are the best, in my opinion.

CHOLESTEROL & CONSTIPATION

Charity Bedell

Although I eat rather healthfully and take care of my body, over the years I have had two health conditions causing me issues. One was a hereditary issue with high cholesterol. The other is an issue with constipation.

To help lower my cholesterol and deal with my constipation issues, I started to eat oatmeal or oat-based cereals. Using this method, I have less issues with constipation and my cholesterol is in the low-to-healthy state for the first time in my life.

COLDS Mistress Belladonna

Here is a "Help Me Honey" remedy for colds and doldrums. First apportion three equal parts of dried elderberries, dried jasmine flowers, and dried mint or orange mint. Sterilize a mason jar and lid by boiling, and, once dry, add equal parts of the herbs into the jar until it is about three-quarters filled. Shake the jar really well. You can also use this time to enchant the herbs with your intent for healing.

Pour in some local honey, making sure that the herbs are completely covered and the jar is full. Once the contents settle, top it off with a little more honey. Heat is not needed for this remedy, but you can heat the jar in a double boiler if you wish. Never boil honey, as it lessens its flavor, and destroys its nutritive aspects. Let the jar sit for at least a week or two in a dark, cool place. The syrup can then be taken as is by spoon, or dissolved in a cup of hot water or tea.

COUGHS Andrea Trendel

For this herbal cough syrup it is better to use fresh herbs that you grind yourself and charge with healing intent, but you can use dried, preground herbs if fresh ones are not available. This syrup is great for easing coughs, combating congestion, and opening sinuses.

Ingredients

- Pinch of clove
- Pinch of rosemary
- Dash of cinnamon
- Dash of ginger
- 1 tablespoon honey
- 1 tablespoon lemon, lime, or pineapple juice
- 1 tablespoon elderberry juice

In a small bowl, mix the herbs with the honey and juices. Note: You can also use 1 teaspoon of cinnamon mixed directly with 1 teaspoon of honey to make an instant syrup. This coats the throat and helps coughs.

Both mixtures are best if slightly heated to add a little warmth to the throat. Take every two to four hours as needed.

CUTS AND SCRAPES Athena Perrakis

Cuts and scrapes are common, and yet they create shifts in our energy fields and serve as invitations to engage healing magick. Sometimes they occur as a way of connecting us with our own blood and life-force magick. In times of injury, I look to the power of the plant kingdom for support. Frankincense, myrrh, wild lavender, calendula, and tea tree essential oils are potent plant and resin allies that you can apply directly to cuts and scrapes (after cleaning them) to activate your innate healing power and quicken your recovery. They also summon healing spirits and guides to surround you as you recover.

DIGESTIVE UPSETS Jasmine Aten

Over the years I have tried many different remedies for digestive upset and have discovered the following to be the most effective, inexpensive, and beneficial natural remedies that use ingredients you probably already have on hand. If not, they can be found for just a couple of dollars at your local grocery store.

Pure aloe vera juice coats the lining of the stomach and intestines to calm acid buildup. **(Note: Do not take digoxin with aloe vera juice, and consult with your health-care practitioner before taking aloe vera juice, as there are numerous contraindications between aloe vera and various conditions and medications.)** Fresh pineapple has enzymes that help break down food for better digestion. Coffee helps food move more quickly through the colon for elimination. And peppermint tea and ginger tea are great for settling an upset stomach. Give one of these natural remedies a try. You will be relieved that you did.

EARACHE Amber Barnes

Here are a couple of witchy tips that may help when you or a loved one has an earache. I remember my grandmother and mother doing these with me.

Drop a tiny bit of warm olive oil in the sore ear, and then place a piece of cotton ball into the ear. I still do this from time to time, but I add essential oils to my olive oil. You can mix 4-6 drops of tea tree or lavender oil to a teaspoon of olive oil and place a few drops on the cotton ball, then insert it into the ear.

I used to swim a lot and was prone to getting swimmer's ear. My grandmother would make a warm compress with a small towel and then have me lay on the couch with my sore ear against the towel. This would help with the pain as well as drain some of the fluids. I still continue with this method today, but I made a flaxseed pillow with essential oils mixed in it. I then heat it up in the microwave for about 15-20 seconds at a time to the desired heat. This can also be done with rice in a clean sock if you don't have time to make a pillow.

FATIGUE Gillian Hughes
How often do you have an energy slump? We often grab a coffee for a sudden rush that doesn't last long, and afterward we feel even more fatigued. Tiredness can be alleviated by using crystal healing to re-energize us. I had one client who was having difficulty coping with chronic fatigue; she was always tired and wasn't sleeping well. I worked on her with high-energy crystals such as red jasper, quartz (smoky, clear, and rose), hematite, and apophyllite to facilitate energy boosts as well as more restful sleep. It was very successful.

FEVER Angela Bass
We release much of our body heat through our skin, so a nice tepid bath will bring down a fever. Please do not plunge into cold water or put ice in the water. The water should be cool—not cold. Another method is to place a cool, damp cloth over your feet. Be sure to drink clear liquids such as water and broth to avoid dehydration. You can also eat frozen seedless grapes or cold watery fruit, such as watermelon, to stay hydrated.

GINGIVITIS Starstone Silvermoon
Here are several solutions for gum pain and gingivitis. The first is a toothpaste. Spoon 1 tablespoon of baking soda, ½ teaspoon of fine rock salt (Himalayan salt is best), and 1 drop of clove oil into a small, shallow screw-top jar. Melt 1 teaspoon of coconut oil and combine with the ingredients in the jar to make a paste. Add more coconut oil if necessary. Use the toothpaste once a week and pull your teeth with pure coconut oil (an Ayurvedic treatment that involves swishing the oil in your mouth for about twenty minutes and then spitting it out) the other days to eliminate your gingivitis.

If your gums bleed, brush them gently with a softer toothbrush and the coconut oil. This will rid the gums of ongoing infection and slough off infected and dead tissue.

Don't forget to floss between your teeth and brush your tongue to rid your mouth of bacteria.

HAIR OILINESS Shawn Robbins

I found that the best solution for oily hair is volcano-ash shampoo, which is found in many online stores. Volcano ash is rich in sulfur and dries out the oily residue, leaving your hair naturally shiny and full of bounce.

HAY FEVER Jane JJ Baxter

I have suffered with hay fever since I was nine years of age. Hay fever can come in different forms, and you can suffer from a multitude of symptoms depending on the time of year. Here are a few remedies to help with those symptoms.

Put a handful of sea salt in your bath and cleanse yourself; this will clear any pollen from your body. I also use a sea-salt nasal spray for a blocked nose; use this 3–4 times a day as needed.

Another way to clear congestion is to put 2–3 drops of eucalyptus oil in water in an oil burner.

For the eyes, soak a cloth in cold water and lay this over your eyes. You can also use cool cucumber slices placed directly on closed eyelids.

For soothing an itchy, sore throat and easing congestion, there are two teas you can make: peppermint tea, and honey and lemon tea. For the first, steep a peppermint tea bag for three minutes in hot water. To make honey and lemon tea, add a slice of lemon and 1 teaspoon of honey to hot water.

HICCUPS Bryant Pinnix

Having hiccups can be quite aggravating. An old folk tale is that when kids have the hiccups, it means that they are growing, but we all know that is simply something our grandparents used to tell us. Hiccups usually occur when we swallow too much air while drinking or eating. It is our body's natural way of saying, "Hey, don't do that!" I have been fortunate enough through the years to have had a few tricks passed down to me for getting rid of those pesky hiccups. I really hope they work for you, too.

Have a friend startle you in some way.

Breath into a paper (not plastic!) bag continuously for about a minute. This raises the amount of carbon dioxide in your lungs and usually stops hiccups.

Finally, my favorite way of all, hold your breath and take several swallows of beer or coke. The fizz will counteract with the air trying to force its way up your throat, and holding your breath makes it impossible to hiccup while you are drinking.

Meanwhile, since I am personally pagan, I would like to leave a little chant that you can have your kids say when they get the hiccups. Who knows? Maybe the words alone will be enough to rid them of those pesky hiccups!

"As above, so below,
hiccups come and they go.
Now they are here and I want them gone,

With the power of air,
hiccups, just leave me alone!
Now thank you, air element, for helping me,
in the name of the goddess."

INSECT BITES AND STINGS

Tamela Farrand

My husband Ron and I are Canadian and have been hand-fasted for twenty-three years. We are the parents of six now-grown children. I was handed this family recipe for a healing salve for bites, stings, cuts, burns and rashes. Always clean the area of skin affected before applying!

Scoop ½ cup (118 ml) of fresh soft shea butter into a large clean bowl. Add 20 drops of plantain essential oil and 10 drops of mullein essential oil. Blend well, then place in a jar with good lid.

If you happen to be camping and left your salve at home, and someone has gotten stung by an insect or spider, go out into the fields and gather some young burdock leaves. Steam them. and use them as a poultice on the bite. Or, if you brought the salve, take 1 teaspoon of it and add the steamed leaves.

Mix well and place some of the mixture on the affected area with a clean cloth wrapped over it to keep it in place. **(Note: Do not use burdock if you are taking medications that slow blood-clotting.)**

I make my own oils, as my grandmother and mom did. Mullein, plantain, and burdock grow wild everywhere where I live, but you can easily purchase them on the Internet. Many blessings from our coven/family to yours!

INSOMNIA Sadie with Sleeping Gryphon

As a business owner, mother, and wise woman, I have been studying witchcraft for the past twenty-three years and herbs for the last ten. I study oneness and try to focus on the bringing together of all people while maintaining our individuality. Here is my "Night-Night Tea" —a remedy for insomnia.

Place the ingredients in a tea infuser and steep for fifteen minutes. Serve with honey, (I use lots to keep up my sweetness!) Drink while warm.

Ingredients

- 3 parts dried chamomile
- 2 parts dried catnip
- 2 parts dried valerian root
- 2 parts dried peppermint
- 1 part dried rose hips

INSOMNIA, SLEEP ISSUES

AnamNa Tine

Many of us suffer from sleep disorders. There are many options out there to help, from drinking warm milk to yoga and meditation to relax the body and mind.

Herbs such as lavender, chamomile, passionflower, hops, lemon balm, and valerian root can help with sleep disorders. **(See pages 212–215 for more information; do not take with sedatives.)**

My favorite sleep chant is:

"The sun is sleeping, the moon is out.
Let the stars guide you through your dream."

KNEE PAIN Alyson Stewart
In 2005, I broke my leg and shattered my ankle. I had multiple breaks and fractures that required surgery. A titanium rod and screws were put in place. Then the healing process began.

As a magickal practitioner and healer, I chose to rely on holistic, natural healing methods. I employed massage and Reiki techniques with healing oils, crystals, and heat to heal and manage pain throughout the process.

Two of my favorite oils for pain relief and management are sweet marjoram and eucalyptus. Sweet marjoram has sedative properties and is helpful with pain and stiffness. (Note: Do not take with lithium.) Eucalyptus oil has analgesic and anti-inflammatory properties to aid in pain relief and swelling. These can be used in massage and Reiki or added to a bath to employ the additional benefits of wet heat.

There are virtually limitless crystal choices for pain relief. My choices are hematite, amethyst, and clear quartz. Hematite reduces pain and increases circulation. Amethyst and clear quartz are for pain relief. Surgical tape can be used to keep the crystals in place on the affected area.

LEG CRAMPS Carmel Norton
Many essential oils have antispasmodic effects, making them effective for leg cramps. To make a simple rubbing oil, combine 2 drops each of marjoram, lavender, and cypress oils in 1 teaspoon of olive oil. Massage into the affected area, rubbing deeply. The combined effect of the oils will increase circulation to the area, releasing the cramp. If you are making a larger amount of oil for future use, store in dark glass bottles in a cool, dark place.

MENSTRUAL CRAMPS Laura Perry
I am a retired naturopath, but even though I'm focusing on writing books and creating tarot art these days, herbalism is still very much a part of my spirituality and my life.

Over the years I have found that a great deal of healing power lurks quietly in our kitchen cupboards, mostly unnoticed. In fact, some of my favorite remedies come from herbs you probably already have in your kitchen. One powerful helper for women is basil, which relieves menstrual cramps with remarkable efficiency.

Place 1 teaspoon of the dried herb in a mug. Pour boiling water over it and then set a saucer on top to hold the steam in while it steeps for ten minutes. Sweeten as desired and thank the plant spirit for the relief.

RAZOR BURN Rev. H.P. Anuj Elvis

Today I am sharing my recipe for soothing razor burn. I always try and keep it simple and like to experiment with ingredients available in my kitchen. Razor burns can be nasty, and my potion is easy yet effective.

What you need are 7 to 8 Indian margosa, or neem, leaves. The quantity depends on how much balm you want to make. Also, 1 teaspoon alum powder and 1 tablespoon honey. Grind the leaves into a paste with your mortar and pestle, and mix all ingredients well. Apply to your beard area—or other shaved areas with razor burn—like a mask, and leave it on for 15 minutes before rinsing off with tap water.

SINUS INFECTIONS Deb Bresser

This is a very good remedy that will work wonders for sinus infections.

Tie together a nice-sized bunch of eucalyptus stems (with leaves) with twine. Hang it from your showerhead and turn the shower on hot. Let a good amount of steam build up, and then adjust the water temperature so you can stand inside the shower. Once you are in the shower, close your eyes to avoid irritation. Breathe the vapor in deeply, and exhale slowly. It will not take long for the mucus to begin to drain. Do this for at least twenty minutes. When you get out of the shower, blow your nose and spit out anything draining down your throat. If you do not have a shower, place the eucalyptus leaves in a pot of boiling water (if you have tea tree oil, you can add that, too—it is a natural antiseptic. Place at least 10–12 drops into the water). I drape a bath towel over my head and the pot and breathe in the steam. Remember to close your eyes to avoid irritation. If you do not feel better after repeating this shower over several days, consult your doctor. Blessings, and stay healthy!

SKIN DRYNESS Opal Seanna Mazza

I was born and raised in the Philippines, where the humidity is so high that dry skin is not a common problem among its citizens. So after I moved to the East Coast of the United States, it took me years to learn how to keep my skin moisturized. Through trial and error, I came up with one of the simplest remedies to combat dry skin, which I am sharing here.

Whisk all the ingredients together in a bowl, then pour into a glass jar. Rub the mixture over your body while in your shower, standing away from the running water. Rinse thoroughly. Do not rub off the water with your towel; just pat down your body to dry. If you do this once or twice a week your skin will feel silky smooth, and you will not need a moisturizer after this treatment.

SKIN IRRITATION Ariel

Plantain oil can be used on many skin irritations, from sunburns to acne to damaged skin. To make an herb-infused oil with plantain, dry fresh plantain leaves by laying them on wax paper and leaving in direct sun. If it is summer, they should be dry by the end of the day—dry a lot to save them for winter. Once dried, add 3-4 cups (96-128 g) dried plantain to your favorite carrier oil (mine is grapeseed oil), using a ratio of 1:2 oil to herb. Place in a dry, cool spot for 3-4 weeks. Strain any leaf bits out with a cheesecloth or strainer. You now have a plantain-infused oil that you can rub into the skin. **(Do not use if you are on warfarin.)**

SPRAINS Mark Bowler

There are two main methods I recommend for relieving sprains: crystal healing, and plants and herbs.

Regarding crystal healing, there are different ideas about which crystals are best for sprains, but I would undoubtedly go for quartz. Most any type of quartz is fine, but the best are clear or rose. Any crystals you use first need to be charged and energized (see pages 72–73), then worn in direct contact with the affected area. They should be recharged after twelve to twenty-four hours. I have found that twenty-four to forty-eight hours is enough to make a significant difference to your pain. You can feel the warmth of the crystals' energy; they are very effective!

For herbs and plants, again, opinions vary, but my tried and tested method is a warm poultice of leopard's bane (*Arnica montana*) and self-heal (*Prunella vulgaris*) applied directly to the affected area. To make the poultice, take a handful of each herb and wrap a piece of muslin around them, securing with a string or cord. Soak the pouch in boiling water for a minute or two, and then remove from the water with tongs or a slotted spoon. Allow it to cool enough so that you can lay it on your skin. After it loses its heat, rewarm it or make a fresh one. They generally can be warmed up three or four times before losing their effectiveness. **(Do not use arnica if you are on medications that slow blood-clotting, and do not use on broken skin.)**

If I had to choose between the two options, I'd go with the poultice—I am old school.

Stay strong! Stay well! So mote it be.

STRESS Kelly Louise Kreqeli

Like many people, I suffer from stress and depression, which causes me to have bad headaches and makes me unable to sleep. I decided to try a natural remedy to reduce my stress levels and depression. I put some lavender oil in an oil diffuser with a white tea-light candle and some light lavender incense sticks. If I do this in my bedroom a few hours before I go to sleep, it really helps. **(Note: Never leave candles or lit incense sticks unattended.)**

Blessed be.

SUNBURN

Dana Kilgore Goudie (Rainwalker Woman)

A mild sunburn has a light-pink color, little pain, and heals fast. Take a cool shower or bath for instant relief. Aloe vera sooths the sting of any burn. Liquid witch hazel is an astringent you should also keep handy. I use witch hazel that has aloe added to it, so I get the benefit of both plants together. Witch hazel is available at most grocery stores and is very inexpensive.

More serious sunburns will be bright red and sometimes blister. Again, a cool shower or bath is helpful. I have also taken vinegar and oatmeal baths to help soothe the pain. I add a cup of apple cider vinegar and/or a cup of oats to the bathwater. Use one or both together, and repeat as necessary.

TOOTHACHE Nanette Baker

Growing up around my maternal grandparents, the herb lore I learned included Native American, Irish, and German traditions.

There are two main herbs I use for toothaches. The first is common clove Grandmother used to place a whole clove between my teeth where the ache was, say "Bite down," and tell me to leave it there until it quit hurting. It was primitive, but it worked. Now I use clove oil. It can be used to numb the gums, and you can put it on a cold sore (where it will burn like fire for half a second and then numb it). I swish with lukewarm saltwater as well, which helps to prevent infection. I **do not recommend using it on children's gums,** because the oil is very strong—especially the smell.

The second herb I use is a plant that is not as well-known: Acmella oleracea, the toothache plant, which is believed to have originated in Brazil. The seeds and leaves have a numbing effect when chewed. A friend introduced me to this plant when I had a toothache one weekend, and it provided relief. I mashed the leaves a little to activate the effect and then pushed them down into the tooth where I had lost a filling and was feeling pain. **(Note: Before chewing toothache plant, discuss with your health-care practitioner, and for serious tooth issues contact your dentist immediately.)**

WINDBURN Terry Fenech

Here is a little home health remedy that is very useful for windburn. In a medium-size bowl, mix 4 teaspoons aloe vera gel or juice, 4 teaspoons rosehip oil, 4 teaspoons borage seed oil (starflower oil can be used instead), 2 tablespoons olive oil, $2/3$ cup (157 ml) cocoa butter, and $1\frac{1}{2}$ tablespoons beeswax. Add a handful of oats and small handfuls of dried chamomile and calendula. Apply the paste to the burn for instant relief.

WRINKLES Lori Morgan

I am going to give you a three-step treatment to naturally reduce inflammation, clean your pores, reduce wrinkles, tighten skin, and shrink large pores. Before beginning any skin-care treatment, always make sure your skin has been properly cleansed with warm water and a facial scrub. You want all dry and dead skin removed.

1. Mint: Boil a handful of mint leaves in water. Strain out the leaves, then drop a piece of clean white cloth into the water.

Let it sit for a few minutes. When the water has cooled slightly but is still warm, take the cloth and gently wring, still leaving some moisture.

Lay the cloth over your face, gently patting. This will open and clean your pores and reduce inflammation.

2. Egg whites: Beat two egg whites in a bowl until they form soft peaks. Using a facial sponge, apply the egg whites to your skin from your chin to your forehead in an upward position, gently massaging them in.

Let the mask sit for twenty minutes, then wash away using a warm cloth, wiping from chin to forehead in an upward position. This will reduce wrinkles and tighten skin and pores.

Let the mask sit for twenty minutes, then wash away using a warm cloth, wiping from chin to forehead in an upward position. This will reduce wrinkles and tighten skin and pores.

3. Witch hazel: Using a facial sponge, apply the witch hazel. Its astringent properties will also tighten your skin.

Regularly using these natural products will help keep your skin healthy.

So mote it be.

Acknowledgments

It takes a village to make a book. At Sterling, we are grateful to our brilliant editor Barbara Berger, who has empowered and inspired us to reach for the stars in writing our book; senior designer Sharon Jacobs, for the stunning design; cover art director Elizabeth Lindy for the beautiful cover design; and production editors Hanna Reich and Kayla Overbey. We also thank Ashley Prine, designer, and Katherine Furman, copyeditor, at Tandem Books, Inc. A special thank-you to Bill Gladstone, our agent, who believed in us.

Of course, there are so many other people whom we should like to thank and acknowledge for their help in making this book a reality. Among these people are Leanna Greenaway, Dru Ann Welch, Rev. Terrie Brookings, and Linda Bedell, who helped with early drafts. We'd also like to thank all of our contributors who have truly made this a book which crosses cultures and connects us across the world.

We also want to thank the founders, administrators, and members of the various Facebook groups that we have learned a lot from. They have encouraged us to reach within ourselves to help you, the reader, along your path. Without all of you, this book would not be possible. We thank you all.

I, Shawn, would also like to acknowledge my dear friend, Timothy Green Beckley—UFO and paranormal pioneer, author, and co-host of *Exploring the Bizarre* on KCOR radio. Our friendship spans many lifetimes of adventure into the unknown and will span many more lifetimes to come.

I, Charity Bedell, want to acknowledge my family: my cousin Donna Norte, who started me on my path as a witch and writer, knowing my gifts from an early age; my mother and father, who taught me to love nature and to find health and wellness within the world around me; and, finally, my loving husband Ben Weston, who has dealt with late nights, stressful days, and the emotional highs and lows through this whole process.

Lastly, as the coauthors of *The Good Witch's Guide*, we would like to acknowledge and thank each other. We have taken from each other wisdom and insight, and vision and clarity, as well as the love of a writing partnership that brings two people together. We share the same hopes and dreams, which are to endeavor to help others obtain wellness in the mind, body, and soul.

RESOURCES

SUPPLIES AND SUPPLIERS

Not everyone wants to or has time to make their own oils or tinctures, or to grow their own herbs. That is perfectly fine. Often it is easier to start out with the work already done for you. This way, you can find what works best for you first.

The following websites are places you can buy all forms of supplies and tools. Some of these sources are general witchcraft, magick, and metaphysical supply shops, and some of them are just for aromatherapy herbs, essential oils, and oil blends.

Essential Oils and Herbs

Herbs & Arts
www.herbsandarts.com/oils

Penn Herb Company
www.pennherb.com

Mountain Rose Herbs
www.mountainroseherbs.com

Monterey Bay Spice Company
www.herbco.com

Eden Botanicals
www.edenbotanicals.com

General Witchcraft and Occult Supplies

Mystic Echoes
www.mystic-echoes.com

Cauldron Craft Odditys
www.etsy.com/shop/CauldronCraftOdditys

HEX: Old World Witchery
www.hexwitch.com

13 Moon
www.13moons.com

AzureGreen
www.azuregreen.net

Hoodoo Supplies

Lucky Mojo
www.luckymojo.com

Original Products Botanica
www.originalbotanica.com

Old Style Conjure
www.oldstyleconjure.com

Voodoo Authentica
www.voodooshop.com/products/index.html

Aromatherapy

Sages Aromatherapy
www.etsy.com/shop/SagesAromatherapy

AromaTools
www.aromatools.com

Dreaming Earth Botanicals
www.dreamingearth.com/catalog/pc/home.asp

RECOMMENDED READING AND REFERENCE MATERIAL

The following books were used as references while writing this text and are
recommended reading for additional research and information.

Magickal Herbalism and Working with Herbs in Magickal and Spiritual Ways

Beyerl, Paul. *A Compendium of Herbal Magic*. Carlsbad, CA: Phoenix Publishing, Inc., 1998.

Casas, Starr. *The Conjure Workbook Volume 1: Working the Root*. Green Valley Lake, CA: Pendraig, 2013.

Cunningham, Scott. *Magical Aromatherapy: The Power of Scent*. Woodbury, MN: Llewellyn, 1989.

———. *Magical Herbalism: The Secret Craft of the Wise*. Woodbury, MN: Llewellyn, 2012.

———. *Cunningham's Encyclopedia of Magical Herbs*. Woodbury, MN: Llewellyn, 1985.

———.*The Complete Book of Incense, Oils & Brews*. Woodbury, MN: Llewellyn, 2002.

Daniel, Marilyn F. *Kitchen Witchery: A Compendium of Oils, Unguents, Incense, Tinctures & Comestibles*. Newburyport, MA: Weiser Books, 2002.

Dugan, Ellen. *Herb Magic for Beginners*. Woodbury, MN: Llewellyn, 2006.

Hopman, Ellen Evert. *A Druid's Herbal of Sacred Tree Medicine*. Rochester, VT: Destiny Books, 2008.

Huson, Paul. *Mastering Herbalism: A Practical Guide*. Lanham, MD: Madison Books, 2001.

Kaldera, Raven. *The Northern Shamanic Herbal*. Hubbardston, MA: Asphodel Press, 2011.

McQuillar, Tayannah Lee. *Rootwork: Using the Folk Magick of Black America for Love, Money, and Success*. New York: Touchstone, 2003.

Papa Jim. *Papa Jim's Herbal Magic Workbook*. Papa Jim, 2001.

Penczak, Christopher, ed. *The Green Lovers: A Compilation of Plant Spirit Magic*. Salem, NH: Copper Cauldron, 2012.

Yronwode, Catherine. *Hoodoo Herb and Root Magic: A Materia Magica of African-American Conjure*. Forestville, CA: Lucky Mojo Curio Company, 2002.

Herbalism for Magick and Health

Beyerl, Paul. *The Master Book of Herbalism*. Blaine, WA: Phoenix Publishing Inc., 1984.

Garrett, J. T. *The Cherokee Herbal: Native Plant Medicine from the Four Directions*. Rochester, VT: Bear & Company, 2003.

Hess, Ray "Doctor Hawk." *Backwoods Shamanism: An Introduction to the Old-Time American Folk Magic of Hoodoo Conjure and Rootwork*. CreateSpace, 2014.

Müller-Ebeling, Claudia, Christian Rätsch, and Wolf-Dieter Storl, PhD. *Witchcraft Medicine: Healing Arts, Shamanic Practices, and Forbidden Plants*. Rochester, VT: Inner Traditions, 2003.

O'Rush, Claire. *The Enchanted Garden: Discovering and Enhancing the Magical Healing Properties in Your Garden*. London: Blandford Press, 1771.

Welch, Dru Ann. *Mama D's Practical Herbal Guide Book: How to Use Herbs in Magick and Healing*. CreateSpace, 2015.

Medicinal Properties of Herbs

Grieve, Mrs. M. *A Modern Herbal: In Two Volumes.* New York: Dover Publications, 1971.

Thomson Healthcare. *PDR for Herbal Medicines, 4th Edition.* Montvale, NJ: Thomson Healthcare Inc., 2007.

Herbal Home Remedies

Breedlove, Greta. *The Herbal Home Spa: Naturally Refreshing Wraps, Rubs, Lotions, Masks, Oils, and Scrubs.* North Adams, MA: Storey, 1998.

Gladstar, Rosemary. *Rosemary Gladstar's Medicinal Herbs: A Beginner's Guide: 33 Healing Herbs to Know, Grow, and Use.* North Adams, MA: Storey, 2012.

———. *Rosemary Gladstar's Herbal Recipes for Vibrant Health: 175 Teas, Tonics, Oils, Salves, Tinctures, and other Natural Remedies for the Entire.* North Adams, MA: Storey Publishing, 2008.

Green, James. *The Herbal Medicine-Maker's Handbook: A Home Manual.* Berkeley, CA: Crossing Press, 2000.

Morrison, Sarah Lyddon. *The Modern Witch's Book of Home Remedies.* New York: Citadel, 1991.

Ody, Penelope. *The Holistic Herbal Directory: A Directory of Herbal Remedies for Everyday Health Problems.* United Kingdom: Ivy Press, 2001.

Todd, Jude C. *Jude's Herbal Home Remedies: Natural Health, Beauty & Home-Care Secrets.* Woodbury, MN: Llewellyn, 2002.

Essential Oils

Harding, Jennie. *The Essential Oils Handbook: All the Oils You Will Ever Need for Health, Vitality, and Well-Being.* United Kingdom: Duncan Baird, 2008.

Schiller, Carol, and David Schiller. *500 Formulas for Aromatherapy: Mixing Essential Oils for Every Use.* New York: Sterling, 1994.

Worwood, Valerie Ann. *The Complete Book of Essential Oils and Aromatherapy.* Novato, CA: New World Library, 2016.

The Magick of Crystals

Cunningham, Scott. *Cunningham's Encyclopedia of Crystal, Gem, and Metal Magic.* Woodbury, MN: Llewellyn Publications, 1998.

Grant, Ember. *The Book of Crystal Spells: Magical Uses for Stones, Crystals, Minerals . . . and Even Sand.* Woodbury, MN: Llewellyn, 2013.

Lecouteux, Claude. *A Lapidary of Sacred Stones: Their Magical and Medicinal Powers Based on the Earliest Sources.* Rochester, VT: Inner Traditions, 2012.

Crystals for Health and Wellness

Gienger, Michael, and Joachim Goebel. *Gem Water: How to Prepare and Use More Than 130 Crystal Waters for Therapeutic Treatments.* Forres, Scotland: Findhorn Press, 2008.

Hall, Judy. *Crystal Prescriptions: The A–Z Guide to Over 1,200 Symptoms and Their Healing Crystals.* Ropley, UK: O Books, 2006.

Harding, Jennie. *Crystals.* Cincinnati: F&W, 2016.

CONTRIBUTORS

Ariel has been practicing naturopathic medecine and homeopathic healing since she was a child, learning from her grandmother.

Jasmine Aten is the founder of the Facebook group "Let's Talk Magick" and owner of www.oneritualaway.com.

Nanette Baker runs the Facebook group "Favorite Online Stores for Witchcraft Items."

Melodie Starr Ball is the creator of the group "Devoted to the Craft" on Facebook.

Amber Barnes is owner of Earth N' Things on Etsy. She is also the creator of "PaganPedia," a fun little group on Facebook where pagan people can learn and grow with one another on their spiritual journey.

Angela Bass is founder of the Facebook group "Pagan Humor."

Jane JJ Baxter is a solitary eclectic witch and psychic medium. She lives in the Algarve, Portugal, with her husband and son. Her Facebook group is "There Is a Little Witch in All of Us."

Yvonne Beaver

Mark Bowler is a landscape gardener and horticulturist. He is founder of the Facebook groups "Pagan/Alternative Market UK" and "Handcrafted Wands." He belongs to several groups, including "Witches in the Hut" and "The Cauldron," a mixing place for witches, druids, and pagans. He follows the Shamanic path.

Deb Bresser is the owner of A Witches Past on Etsy.

Ginger Burkey

Liz Carney is administrator for "Witches Coven" and "Witches Gathering" sites on Facebook.

Derrie P. Carpenter is the creator of the group "Pagan and Proud" on Facebook.

Kimberlie Miller Clark is a third-generation healer.

Kenya Coviak, aka Mistress Belladonna, has been a teacher and writer in Michigan for several years. She is the founder of the Black Moon Tradition/Grove and the "Detroit Paganism Examiner" on Facebook, a freelance contributor to several publications, and a board member for Pagan Pride Detroit and the Universal Society of Ancient Ministry. Kenya is also the chief editor of the PBN News Network. She follows the Sacred Fool.

Cheryl Croce Culver is the founder of "The Crafty Kitchen WITCH" on Facebook.

Rev. H.P. Anuj Elvis is an eclectic practitioner of the craft and the founder of the nonprofit organization Earth Temple, India, which is run by the members of the Coven of Hecate's Kin (C.O.H.K) and managed by Mannsha Solutions, India, which can be reached at Covenofhecateskin@gmail.com. He is also the founder of the Facebook group "Witchcraft and Magick."

Tamela Farrand is Hereditary High Priestess of the Sacred Circle of Ancient Wisdom Hearthstone Covenstead.

Terry Fenech is the owner of craftingmagic.co.uk.

Chianne Frasure is co-founder of "Pink Moon Pagan Place" on Facebook alongwith Stacy Griffing.

Dana Kilgore Goudie (Rainwalker Woman) is the creator of a Facebook page titled "Rainwalker's Magickal Path."

Leanna Greenaway is a columnist for *Fate & Fortune* magazine, UK; author of *Simply Wicca* and *Simply Tarot*, and co-author of *Wiccapedia: A Modern-Day White Witch's Guide*.

Angel Greer is the creator of two groups on Facebook: "Pagans of the Path" and "Bits and Pieces of Pagan Pride."

Lori Hayes, aka Darklady, is a solitary witch, psychic, medium, and empath. She is the creator of numerous Facebook pages, including "Darkladys Horror Halloween."

Gillian Hughes is the owner of "Cornish Crystal Cavern" on Facebook and at www.cornishcrystalcavern.co.uk.

Charissa Iskiwitch (Lady Charissa) has been working as a healer for over twenty-five years, using a variety of healing methods, including energy, herbs, and crystal healing. She provides life coaching, is a Reiki master and practitioner of Southern Appalachian folk remedies, and is the creator of the Charissa's Cauldron line of natural remedies, charissascauldron.com. She is also the founder of the Pagan Business Network, paganbusinessnetwork.com.

Rob Jones is cofounder of the Facebook group "Practitioners of the Craft" with John "Tip" Massaro.

Karen Kasinskas runs the Facebook group "Wicca Talk" and is the headmaster of a coven. Her goal is to reach as many people as possible and spread the joy and love of being Wiccan and pagan.

Kelly Louise Kreqeli is the founder of the Facebook group "Wiccapedia."

Connie Lavoie considers herself a creator of "Wiccan/Pagan Group for Beginners" on Facebook and a non-British traditional witch. She was born and raised in Connecticut, resides in southeastern Tennessee, and has been practicing on and off for about fifteen years.

Bronwyn Le Fae, of www.charmedbystarr.com, is treasurer of the Wiccan Family Temple.

Opal Seanna Mazza is an Usai and Kundalini Reiki master healer/teacher, Integrated Energy® therapist, chakra healer, crystal healer, and master diviner. She also owns a small online store on Etsy, House of Unicorn Opal, where most items she sells are her own work and crafts.

Dr. Kimberly S. McAfee founded the blog christopagankim.wordpress.com/.

Rachel McGirr is the creator of "The Witches Lair" on Facebook.

Jamie Mendez is the founder of Magickal Me and Awakening the Divine Feminine workshops.

Donna Morgan is the founder of several Facebook groups, including "Legion of Pagans of the Old Ways."

Lori Morgan is owner of "The Witch's Nook" on Facebook and Twitter.

Ceane O'Hanlon-Lincoln is author of the Sleuth Sisters Mysteries series. She has both a personal page and a Sleuth Sisters Mysteries page on Facebook.

Carmel Norton is owner of Crystal Hart & Soul on Facebook and Etsy.

Stevie Papoi is owner of Candles by Stevie on Facebook. As a Wiccan, he likes to put his skills as a candlemaker and teacher to use by helping people learn about the New Age path. Connecting with his local community is very important to him.

Sunbow Pendragon is the author of the Black Knight of Avalon Chronicles and is the owner and operator of Amethyst Free Press on Facebook.

Athena Perrakis owns the metaphysical shop and showroom www. sagegoddess.com.

Laura Perry is a retired naturopath. Although she is currently focusing on writing books and creating tarot art, herbalism is still very much a part of her spirituality and her life. You can find her books and tarot deck at www.LauraPerryAuthor.com.

Bryant Pinnix is an administrator of "The Eclectic Circle of Pagans" group on Facebook.

Cary Pizarro is the owner of Le Krem, a natural skin-care products store on Facebook.

Sadie is a co-owner of the Sleeping Gryphon metaphysical shop (sleepinggryphon.net/), a mother, and a wise woman. She has been studying witchcraft for the past twenty-three years and herbs for the last ten. She studies oneness and tries to focus on the bringing together of all people while maintaining our individuality.

Sheila Sager

Sherry, aka Phoenix Rayn Song, is "Witches Forum" on Facebook.

Starstone Silvermoon, a natural male witch, energy healer, and father of five boys, is originally from Colorado and married to poetic flame.

Katie Snow is the creator and founder of the group "The Spellery" and *Spellery Magazine* on Facebook.

Alyson Stewart is the creator of the group "Magickal Inquiry" and the page "Regal Mystic" on Facebook.

Sherry Tapke

AnamNa Tine is the founder of three groups on Facebook: "Native American Witches," "Anam Na Tine," and "Magical Witchcraft." "Anam Na Tine" means "soul of fire." She has been practicing witchcraft for over twenty years, working in many areas but mostly in hemomancy (blood magic), druidism, and love magic.

Andrea Trendel is owner of Soul Coven, Triple Moon Goddess Coven, and more. She is a thirteenth generation witch and high priestess. She loves to teach those who have an interest in learning.

Robert Vilches—aka Reverend Raven Nightclaw, H.P.—is an "unconventional tarot reader" and Reiki master.

Yancy Walker is the creator of "Wicca Craft of the Wise" on Facebook.

Dru Ann Welch is a teacher and the author of *Mama D's Practical Herbal Guide Book*. She found her path to Wicca and witchcraft in 2002.

Angela Scheppler Whiteman

Lashette Williams is owner of Scarlet Moon Creations, a natural bath and body products shop on Etsy. She is a neophyte in the Songs of the Woode coven of Celtic Traditionalist Gwyddonaid and has been on the pagan path since 2003.

Heidi Wolfson

Tracie (Sage) Wood is an aromatherapist and instinctive natural healer, using essential oils as her medium. She owns the store Sage's Aromatherapy & Oils on Facebook and Etsy, which helps people with such ailments as fibromyalgia, arthritis, migraines, depression, bronchial, and sleep issues.

INDEX

PICTURE CREDITS